The Days of the 7th Angel

A Volume of the Eschatology Series

By Donald Peart

- *The New King James is the Bible translation used, unless otherwise noted.*
- *All bold text and literal parenthetical phrases in the Scripture references are added by the author for clarity.*
- *Dictionary reference, includes, but not limited to, Strong's Concordance, BibleWorks Software, and ISA2 Basic Software*

Cover Design: Donald Jr and Jeshua Peart

ISBN: 978-0-9852481-2-3

Acknowledgments

In sincere appreciation, I credit the Holy Spirit who provided the revelation which is set forth in this book. I also acknowledge two men of God, among many, who have imparted to me important concepts acknowledged in this book, Dr. Kelley Varner of Richland North Carolina, and Dr. Joshua (Turnel) Nelson of Trinidad & Tobago, both of whom are with the Lord Jesus.

Table of Content

Introduction 1

Who Introduces the 7th Angel? 3

The Angel, His Roar and the Sea 7

The Seven Thunders 11

Adoptions ("Placed-Sons") 16

The Spirit of the "Placed-Son" 16

The 7th Angel, the Interruption 29

The Mystery of God is Finished 37

The Days of the 7th Angel 45

Who are the Seven Angels? 57

Introduction

In April 2011, I taught most of the message in this book at one of our leadership class. After, the class I really felt impressed to put this understanding in a book. As I was meditating that Monday night on what to title this book, I heard a voice inside of me say call it: **"The days of the Seventh Angel."**

The title seems to fit with regards to what I was teaching in the leadership class, hence this little book. There are so many questions about the seven seals and the seven trumpets that are a result of the seventh seal, and the angel associated with each trumpet. Thus, my intent is to give some clarity, per revelation the Lord has given me.

I did not encumber this little book with too many extensive details. I also did not "exhaust" the "topics" related to the seventh trumpet (i.e., the resurrection of the two witnesses ("first-fruit Christ," the comings (plural) of the Lord, etc.). Thus, the reader should employ his/her spiritual intelligence of understanding as enhanced by the Holy Spirit. The reader is also welcomed to send us any questions he/she may have to the email or to the address given at the end of this book.

With that said, the seventh angel with his trumpet is the last angel of the second group of seven angels[1] each of which were given a trumpet (watchmen with a clear prophetic message) to voice. I could discuss all the previous six angels with their trumpets according to what the Lord have shown me; and for clarity, I do not believe that the understanding given me is absolute, because revelation knowledge is also progressive.

All of us only have "a part." However, if we learn to listen to each other, by stopping doctrinal protectionism, and doctrinal superiority the "whole" "showbread" can be eaten as distributed

---

[1] The sets of seven angels are: the seven angels of the seven Churches *(Revelation 1:20);* the seven angels with seven trumpets *(Revelation 8:2);* and the seven angels with the seven last plagues *(Revelation 15:1)*

by the Son of God, the Lord Jesus Christ, as well as the Father's other legitimate sons and daughters. With that said, the **days** of the seventh trumpet happened, are happening, and will happen again, until the change comes in our "eye" and in our "atoms."

Blessings,

Donald Peart, called to be a son of the Heavenly Father.

Who Introduces the 7th Angel?

Revelation 10:1-7a: *¹I saw still another **mighty angel** coming down from heaven, clothed with **a cloud.** And a **rainbow** was on his head, his face was like the **sun,** and his feet like **pillars of fire**... ⁵The angel whom I saw standing on the sea and on the land raised up his hand to heaven ⁶and swore by Him who lives forever and ever ... that there should be delay no longer, ⁷but in the days of the sounding of the seventh angel ....*

In the beginning of the book of Revelation, John, the beloved apostle stated that the book of Revelation is the "Revelation of Jesus Christ." Thus, when we interpret the book of Revelation, we must be diligent to know that Jesus is involved in every part of the book. The book of Revelation is about Jesus and His Church consisting of the believing Jews and the believing Gentiles. With that understood, the book of the Revelation of Jesus Chris is foremost about Jesus. The "Mighty Angel" who introduces the seventh angel who had the seventh trumpet is representative of Jesus. Jesus does appear in different forms **(Mark 16:12)!** Men are also called angels.[2] Jesus calls His apostles angels **(Luke 9:52-54).** The Bible calls prophets "angels;" and priests are also called messengers (lit., angels) **(Malachi 2:7).** The prophet Malachi called John, the Baptist an angel. Malachi also called Jesus "the Angel."

Malachi 3:1: *"Behold, I send **My messenger (lit. my angel),** And he will prepare the way before Me. And the Lord, whom you seek, will suddenly come to His temple, Even **the Messenger (lit., the Angel) of the covenant,** in whom you delight. Behold, He is coming," Says the LORD of hosts.*

Luke 7:26-28: *²⁶But what went ye out to see? a prophet? Yea, I say unto you, and much more than a prophet. ²⁷This is he of whom it is written, Behold, I send **my messenger** before thy face, who shall prepare thy way before thee. ²⁸I say unto you, among them that are born of women there is none greater than **John:** yet he that is but little in the kingdom of God is greater than he.*

---

[2] Refer to the last chapter of this book for further explanation of this principle.

It is clear from the references that "my messenger" is John, the Baptist, as also witnessed by the Lord Jesus Himself. In addition, "the Messenger of the Covenant" is Jesus, whom Malachi called "the Lord." As it is written: "And **the Lord** who you seek ...even **the Messenger** of the covenant." Jesus is "the Lord." Jesus is also "the Angel (Messenger) who suddenly came to His temple." Thus, it is my understanding that the "Mighty Angel" in **Revelation 10:1** is Jesus who is the Angel of the New Covenant. Let us look at the proofs. This "Mighty Angel" was "clothed with **a cloud**," or literally "clothed with **cloudiness.**" This "cloud" or "cloudiness" surrounding the "Mighty Angel" also means that the "glory" of the Father is testifying that this "Mighty Angel is His Son, Jesus, whom we must "hear."

2 Chronicles 5:13-14: *[13]Indeed it came to pass, when the trumpeters and singers were as one, to make one sound to be heard in praising and thanking the LORD, and when they lifted up their voice with the trumpets and cymbals and instruments of music, and praised the LORD, saying: "For He is good, For His mercy endures forever," that the house, the house of the LORD, was filled with a **cloud**, [14]so that the priests could not continue ministering because of the **cloud; for the glory** of the LORD filled the house of God.*

Luke 9:34-36: *[34]While he was saying this, a **cloud** came and overshadowed them; and they were fearful as they entered the cloud. [35]And a **voice** came out of the **cloud, saying, "This is My Beloved Son. Hear Him!"** [36]When the voice had ceased; **Jesus** was found alone....*

The cloud covering Jesus, the Mighty Angel, in **Revelation 10:1** is a symbol showing that "the Father of Glory" is testifying out of the cloud that this "Mighty Angel" is indeed His "Beloved Son;" and all needs to "hear" His "Son." This can mean that all this Angel said, as the Son of God, is very, important; and we will learn that His message is also about God's other sons to be "placed" as mature sons. The Rainbow on the head of Jesus, the Mighty Angel, is a symbol of the Everlasting Covenant instituted through Jesus (remember the rainbow was God's sign to Noah of God's covenant with Noah); the rainbow on the Mighty Angel's head is also a symbol of the "manifold (lit., **many colored**) wisdom of God;" and "the 'many colored' grace of God" **(Genesis 9:13; Ephesians 3:10, 1 Peter 4:10).**

The Mighty Angel's "face was like **the sun.**" In the New Testament, Jesus' face is compared to the "sun." Again, this is a symbol of the illumination that comes from the face of Jesus. The "Son" will shine in His "strength" or "power" during the days of the seventh angel, who sounds the seventh trumpet. That is, Jesus' power will be manifesting in the earth through God's many sons.

Matthew 17:1-2: ¹*Now after six days Jesus took Peter, James, and John his brother, led them up on a high mountain by themselves;* ²*and He was transfigured before them.* **His face shone like the sun,** *and His clothes became as white as the light.*

Revelation 1:16: He had in His right hand seven stars, out of His mouth went a sharp two-edged sword, and His countenance was **like the sun** *shining in its* **strength (lit., power).**

2 Corinthians 4:6: For it is the God who commanded light to shine out of darkness, who has **shone in our hearts** *to give the light of the knowledge of the glory of God* **in the face of Jesus Christ.**

The face of the Mighty Angel shining as the sun represents "the light of the knowledge of God's glory in the face of Jesus Christ." Jesus is full of the knowledge of the glory of God. Jesus face also illuminates the world with this same knowledge. Per **Matthew 17:2**, the Angel's face shining as the sun, tells us this Mighty Angel is in a transfigured (glorified) state. The sun also represents the manifestation of Jesus' "power" to the earth and sea. The "two pillars of fire" draws from the days of Moses, when the Lord guided the children of Israel with the cloud by day and the pillar of fire by night. *"And the LORD went before them by day in a* **pillar of** *cloud to lead the way, and by night in a* **pillar of fire** *to give them* **light,** *so as to go by day and night." (Exodus 13:21).*

This tells me that **Revelation 10** also occurs during the night season. Jesus will manifest His feet as pillars of fire (a "light" to

His people on the "earth," a light to the "sea" of humanity in the night season) for the Israel of God (His Church) to continue moving towards becoming mature sons of glory in the earth. Finally, the Mighty Angel is also shown to be Jesus by the fact that He uttered an oath. We are specifically instructed not to take an oath. However, the Mighty Angel, Jesus took an oath by the greater One, the Father, as he did in **Daniel 12.**

Matthew 5:33-37: [33]*"Again you have heard that it was said to those of old, 'You shall not **swear** falsely, but shall perform your oaths to the Lord.'* [34]*"But I say to you, do not **swear** at all: neither by heaven, for it is God's throne;* [35]*"nor by the earth, for it is His footstool; nor by Jerusalem, for it is the city of the great King.* [36]*"Nor shall you **swear** by your head, because you cannot make one hair white or black.* [37]*"But let your 'Yes' be 'Yes,' and your 'No,' 'No.' For whatever is more than these is from the evil one."*

Only God and His Son, Jesus may establish an oath that is good. "For when God made a promise to Abraham, because He could **swear** by **no one greater, He swore** by Himself ...." **(Hebrews 6:13-14).** Jesus, the Mighty Angel swore by the "greater One," His Father who lives forever. This is the oath He took: "Time (Chronos **(uninterrupted time)** shall be no longer." Time as we know it will be **interrupted** by the seventh angel. The Mighty Angel, Jesus, took an oath indicating that "chronos will <u>not</u> continue as it is." Time will be interrupted. It is an oath that cannot be broken. The oath cannot be broken or changed. Oaths are immutable; and God cannot lie **(Hebrews 6: 17-18)!** The Lord will interrupt time. The seventh angel will trumpet; and the mystery of God (the mystery of Christ[3] and of the Father) will be completed in His people in the earth.

---

[3] The mystery of Christ also involves some in the Church coming into the faith and knowledge that a corporate Christ (a corporate son in the Father of our Lord Jesus) will arise in the earth to walk as Jesus, the Son of God walked (Ephesians 4:13, John 17:21-26, 1 Corinthians 12:12, Galatians 3:26-27, 1 Corinthians 15:23 (as written in the Greek text), Luke 4:41, Revelation 11),

The Angel, His Roar, and the Sea

Revelation 10:1-3: [1]*I saw still another* **mighty angel** *coming down from heaven ....* [2]*He had a little book open in his hand. And he set his right foot on* **the sea** *and his left foot on the land,* [3]*and* **cried with a loud voice, as when a lion roars.**

In the verses above, we see another witness that shows that the Mighty Angel is Jesus. Jesus is the Lion of the tribe of Judah **(Revelation 5:5).** It was the Lion/Lamb who took the book out of the right hand of Him who sits on the Throne **(Revelation 5:7).** In **Revelation 10:3,** this Lion/Lamb still has the book in His right hand, except He is now in the form of a Mighty Messenger **who roars;** and the book is now open; because the seven seals were already loosed and/or opened by Him **(see Revelation 6:12).**

With the open book in His right hand, Jesus, the Lion of the tribe of Judah, "cried with a loud voice, as when **a lion roars."** The "lion's roar" has many significations. His roar may mean that He has taken prey (the earth and the sea) **(Amos 3:4 w/Revelation 10:2-3).** The Lions roar also points to the "trumpet" that brings "fear" **(Amos 3:4 w/3:6).**

The lion's roar also points to "prophecy" after the Lord has spoken to His servants concerning the secret of Jesus **(Amos 3:8).** The lions roar can also mean the "kings' wrath" **(Proverbs 19:12).** All these points have meaning, yes! **But the Father and the Lord Jesus is after "sons" and "daughters."**

The Mighty Angel's roar also called sons of God from the "sea" of humanity, as we will see in a moment. (The "sea" is also a symbol of troubled humanity **(Isaiah 57:20).)** In the days of the voice of the seventh angel, as Jesus claims the earth and the sea by placing His feet of ownership on the earth and the sea, Jesus will be calling sons from the sea of humanity and the earth. In other words, our Lord Jesus Christ through His roar, as a lion, will save people from sea of humanity and convert them to **"become** sons of God." He is and will be doing the same for the "earth." That is, according to

Daniel 7:3 and Daniel 7:17, the sea and the earth can be synonymous. He is not willing that any should perish, but that all would come to repentance **(2 Peter 3:9).**

Jesus will place His foot on the sea of humanity and the earth dweller in conquest. He will roar like a lion; that is, He will cause His fear to be felt in the earth and the sea. He will call sons and daughters from the sea of humanity through His "Greater Light" of His face (the power of the sun); His light from His feet (the pillar of fire), and through the rousing call of His roar.

*Hosea 11:10: They shall walk after **Jehovah, who will roar like a lion;** for **he will roar,** and the **children (lit., sons)** shall come trembling from the **west (lit., sea).***

Before I discuss Hosea 11: cited above, let me reiterate that **Revelation 10,** points to "sonship," or the placing of God's sons (one of the three phases of "adoption" (son-placing). **Revelation 10** points to Jesus the "only begotten Son;" and **Revelation 10** also points to the "many sons" that the Father will "lead into glory." Remember, we learned in the previous chapter that the Mighty Angel, Jesus, was clothed with a cloud that relates to God confirming Jesus as the Son.

That is, we learned from Apostle Peter that on the Holy Mount, the Father spoke out of the cloud that enveloped Jesus giving Him "glory and honor," declaring that Jesus is indeed His "Beloved Son;" and that we ought to "hear Him." Thus, the Mighty Angel being clothed with a cloud is a symbol of the glory of Jesus as the "placed" mature Son (Sonship).

It follows that when the angel put his feet of pillars of fire on the sea and the earth, Jesus' "Light" and fire was given to those in the sea and earth. Those of the sea believed in that Light and followed that Light becoming "sons" unto God as Hosea 11:10 indicated **(John 1:4 w/1:12).** Those of the earth will hear the God of glory thunder and will leave "kindred" and **"country (lit., earth)"** to become sons of God **(Acts 7:1-3).**

The Lion of the Tribe of Judah roared as His feet of pillars of fire were giving His Light to the sea of humanity and the earth. As Hosea said, "The '**sons**' shall come trembling from the '**sea.**'" Halleluiah! Sons shall leave their natural kin and their "earth-country" to become sons of the "Father-land" **(Hebrews 11:14)**. God wants to "bring many sons to glory" **(Hebrews 2:10)**. He will place sons from the earth and the sea, as the follow the Light of Jesus into maturity.

The days of the sounding of the seventh angel are days of the manifestation of the sons of God. The sons of God will interrupt time as we know it. Salvation shall come to those who are considered morally wrong in the sea.

*Isaiah 57:20: But the **wicked** are like the **troubled sea**, when it cannot rest, whose waters cast up mire and dirt.*

The wicked are like a "troubled sea." "Trouble," per Strong's Concordance, means to be **driven out from one's possession,** it also means to divorce or expatriate (to deport). The word "wicked" means to be morally wrong, to disturb, to violate, condemned, to make trouble.

The fact that Jesus put His feet of the pillar of fire on the "sea" has two meanings. The "violators" of the sea of humanity who reject His Light (the pillar of fire) will be "driven out from their possession" **(compare Genesis 3:24)**. Yet, there is also a positive view about His feet being placed on the sea of humanity. This view is that God is calling many sons from the troubled sea of humanity; and I believe this view of God, the Father, calling many sons from the sea to be God's will.

Those who believe in His Light will be restored their possessions (inheritance) as sons of God, which was the Heavenly Father's original intent for humanity. The "divorce" from God that is prevalent in the sea of humanity will be reversed. The elements of the world will be interrupted. Those who follow His Light will be joined to His Light. They will become sons of God. The Lord "will let them dwell in **their houses.**" They will be restored their inheritance that pertains to **sons (Galatians 4:1-7).** Yes, the Lion of the tribe of Judah shall roar, and many in the sea of humanity and the earth shall become sons of God.

*Hosea 11:10-11: [10]They shall walk after **Jehovah, who will roar like a lion;** for **he will roar,** and the **children (lit., sons)** shall come trembling from the **west (lit., sea).** [11]They shall come trembling like a bird from Egypt, Like a dove from the land of Assyria. **And I will let them dwell in their houses,"** Says the LORD.*

The Seven Thunders

Revelation 10:1-3: *¹I saw still another mighty angel coming down from heaven … ³and cried with a loud voice, as when a lion roars. When he cried out,* **seven thunders uttered their voices.**

The seven thunders are also linked to God interrupting time (chronos) by **"placing"** sons. The Greek word for the phrase "adoption as sons" used in the New Testament literally means: "sons-**placed**," or "**to place** as sons."

The theme of **Revelation 10** and the voice of the seventh angel also involve **"sonship"** — the placing of sons. This theme of sonship is also voiced in the seven thunders who uttered their voices when the Mighty Angel, Jesus, roared as a lion. Let us look at this truth in detail.

First, I must acknowledge that when John heard the voices of the seven thunders and was about to write what the seven thunders said, he was instructed not to write what the thunders uttered. *"Now when the seven thunders uttered their voices,* **I was about to write; but I heard a voice from heaven saying to me, "Seal up the things which the seven thunders uttered, and do not write them"** *(Revelation 10:4).*

Thus, many, including myself, have thought that whatever was said by the seven thunders was sealed with John forever. However, the seal is the Spirit **(Ephesians 1:13).** Thus, the Lamb of God through the Holy Spirit can reveal the sayings of the seven thunders as His will **(Revelation 5:1-5).**

Ephesians 3:1-5: *¹For this reason I, Paul, the prisoner of Christ Jesus for you Gentiles — ²if indeed you have heard of the dispensation of the grace of God which was given to me for you, ³how that* **by revelation** *He made known to me the mystery (as I have briefly written already, ⁴by which, when you read, you may understand my knowledge in the mystery of Christ), ⁵which in other ages was not made known to the sons of men, as it has* **now** *been revealed by* **the Spirit** *to His holy apostles and prophets.*

There are some mysteries about Jesus Christ and His Church that was once hidden in other ages; *"the mystery which has been hidden from **ages** and from **generations**, but now has been revealed to His saints" (**Colossians 1:26**).* The Holy Spirit is now revealing some of those things that were once "unlawful" to repeat or write, just as Jesus legalized, in His days as the Son of Man, things that were once unlawful **(Luke 6:1-7).**

*2 **Corinthians** 12:3-4:* *³And I know such a man – whether in the body or out of the body I do not know, God knows – ⁴how he was caught up into Paradise and heard inexpressible words, which it is **not lawful** for a man to utter.*

Paul like John was restricted during their day to repeat certain things they heard in the Spirit. In the case of Paul, he heard "inexpressible words" in the third heaven which were "not lawful for a man to utter." John heard the voices of seven thunders which he was not permitted to repeat at the time he heard it. Daniel was also told that some of the words he had heard were sealed **"until the time of the end" (Daniel 12:9).**

I am amazed at the level of revelation knowledge that the apostle Paul received, even though he did not physically walk with the Lord like the twelve apostles of the Lamb (Peter, James, John, Andrew, etc.). However, as we just read in Ephesians and Colossians cited earlier, **Paul in all his understanding has made it clear to us that God seals some revelation from one age and from one generation to reveal that mystery in another age and to another generation.**

Jesus himself did things that were once unlawful. He indicated that the saints can also partake of things which were once thought to be unlawful. Working on the Sabbath was once unlawful. Picking corn on the Sabbath was once unlawful, eating priest bread was once unlawful, etcetera.

Matthew 12:1-8: *¹At that time Jesus went through the grain fields on the Sabbath. And His disciples were hungry and began to pluck heads of grain and to eat. ²And when the Pharisees saw it, they said to Him, "Look,* *your disciples are doing what is **not lawful** to do on the Sabbath!"* ³*But He said to them, "Have you not read what David did when he was hungry, he and those who were with him:* ⁴*"how he entered the house of God and ate the **showbread** which was **not lawful** for him to eat, nor for those who were with him, but only for the priests?* ⁵*"**Or have you not read in the law that on the Sabbath the priests in the temple profane the Sabbath, and are blameless?** ⁶"Yet I say to you that in this place there is **One greater than the temple**.* ⁷*"But if you had known what this means, 'I desire mercy and not sacrifice,' you would not have condemned the guiltless.* ⁸*"**For, the Son of Man is Lord even of the Sabbath."***

Jesus made it clear that some things that were once labeled to be "unlawful" are now "lawful." We can eat from the **"showbread."** The word "showbread" is also translated as "purpose" in **Ephesians 1:11, Ephesians 3:11, 2 Timothy 1:9,** and so on. At one time **"purpose"** (showbread) was unlawful; however, through Jesus, whatever is "purposed" to be known through the bread of His word is now lawful. We can now partake of our purpose — our "pre-placement" in Christ, through Jesus Christ, as God's sons.

Our "pre-placement" is to be "placed" as mature sons ("adoption as sons"). God's purposes (lit., pre-place) allow for that which was once off limits to be now accessible. "In Him also, we have obtained an inheritance, being **predestined** according to the **purpose (lit., "showbread," or "preplaced")** of Him who works all things according to the counsel of His will" **(Ephesians 1:11).** That is, we are part of the showbread, the purpose of God. We are not accidents. We are bread to be eaten by others to give life to them.

With that said, the voice of the seven thunders can be understood through the Holy Spirit. On July 1, 2008, the Lord began to give me an understanding about the seven thunders; and I repeat, He only gave me **"an"** understanding. As Job said, we are only on the edges of his ways.

Here is what I received. The seven thunders uttered their "voices." Thus, there are seven "voices" of thunders. These seven voices are seen in **Psalm 29**. In **Psalm 29,** the seven voices of the seven thunders are called the "voice(s) of the Lord."

Psalm 29:1-11, *A Psalm of David: ¹Give unto the LORD, O you mighty ones, Give unto the LORD glory and strength. ²Give unto the LORD the glory due to His name; Worship the LORD in the beauty of holiness. ³The* ***voice of the LORD*** *is over the waters;* ***The God of glory thunders;*** *The LORD is over many waters. ⁴****The voice of the LORD*** *is powerful;* ***The*** ***voice of the LORD*** *is full of majesty. ⁵****The voice of the LORD*** *breaks the cedars, Yes, the LORD splinters the cedars of Lebanon. ⁶He makes them also skip like a calf, Lebanon and Sirion like a young wild ox. ⁷****The*** ***voice of the LORD divides*** *the flames of fire. ⁸****The voice of the LORD*** *shakes the wilderness; The LORD shakes the Wilderness of Kadesh. ⁹****The*** ***voice of the LORD*** *makes the deer give birth and strips the forests bare; And in His temple, everyone says, "Glory!" ¹⁰The LORD sat enthroned at the Flood, And the LORD sits as King forever. ¹¹The LORD will give strength to His people; The LORD will bless His people with peace.*

David gave a key to understanding the seven thunders. David, as we will see in a moment, also defined what the seven thunders uttered. In **Psalm 29:3**, "the voice of the Lord" is defined as the "God of glory" who "thunders." Thus, the voice of the Lord repeated seven times in **Psalm 29** is the God of glory thundering; and He is thundering a message. However, before we discuss the message let us see the effects or the workings of the voices of the seven thunders.

1. The voice of the LORD is over the waters

2. The voice of the LORD is powerful

3. The voice of the LORD is full of majesty

4. The voice of the LORD breaks the cedars

5. The voice of the LORD divides the flames of fire

6. The voice of the LORD shakes the wilderness

7. The voice of the LORD makes the deer give birth

Remember now that the "voice of the Lord" is "the God of glory thunders." Thus, God's "seven thunders" are seen in the seven voices of **Psalm 29. Psalm 29** gives the effects or the working of the seven thunders who uttered their voices. With that said, "What did the God of glory say in His seven thunders?" Here are the answers the Lord revealed to me, as outlined by David in **Psalm 29.**

Psalm 29:1-2, A Psalm of David: [1]Give unto the LORD, O you mighty ones, Give unto the LORD glory and strength. [2] Give unto the LORD the glory due to His name; Worship the LORD in the beauty of holiness.

The word "give" used in verse 1 and 2 is also translated as "ascribe," "to set," or "put," and better yet, the word also means **"to place."** The word "mighty" is translated as **"God"** as used in **Genesis 14:18** indicating that Melchizedek was "a priest of **God** Most High;" and the Hebrew word for "O you … ones" is literally **"sons."**

Thus, **Psalm 29:1-3** reads as such: *"Place to the Lord sons of God," place to the Lord glory and strength, place to the Lord the glory due to His name; worship the Lord in the decorations of holiness. The voice of the Lord is over the waters; the God of Glory thunders …."*

What was the voice of the Lord saying? The voice of the Lord, which is the voices of the seven thunders, is thundering **"place to the Lord sons of God!"** Herein is an understanding of what the seven thunders uttered in **Revelation 10.** The seven thunders declared it's the season to "interrupt time" to "place sons of God unto the Lord." They are to interrupt "time" as Jesus, their Greater brother, interrupted time outlined in **Galatians 4:1-7 and Matthew, Mark, Luke, John, and Acts.** These "sons of God" are of the Melchizedek order of priests. The Melchizedek priesthood is equated to being placed sons of God **(Hebrews 5:6-7).** Paul in the New Testament calls this "placing of sons," "adoption."

*Hebrews 5:5-6: [5]So also Christ did not glorify Himself to become **High Priest,** but it was He who said to Him: **"You are My Son,** Today I have begotten You." [6]As He also says in another place: "You are **a priest forever** according to the **order of Melchizedek"***

Adoptions ("Placed-Sons")

Ephesians 1:3-6: *³Blessed be the God and Father of our Lord Jesus Christ, who has blessed us with every spiritual blessing in the heavenly places in Christ, ⁴just as He chose us in Him before the foundation of the world, that we should be holy and without blame before Him in love, ⁵having* **predestined us to adoption as sons** *by Jesus Christ to Himself, according to the good pleasure of His will, ⁶to the praise of the glory of His grace, by which He has made us accepted in the Beloved.*

In the verses above Paul stated that the Father has "blessed us with every spiritual blessing in the heavenly places in Christ." He then provided a list of some of these blessings — He chose us in Christ before the world was founded; we are holy and without blame before Him in love (His love); "we are into the praise of His glory," **we are predestined "to adoption as sons."** "Adoption as sons" literally reads **"placed as sons."** Therefore, we are "predefined" to be "placed sons."

"Adoption" as used in the Bible is not to be understood from a western point of view. In the west, we understand adoption as one who is parentless, and thus can be adopted by a non-biological parent. Adoption in the Bible means that a person is a biological son who is now matured to be "placed" as a son to bear his father's name, speak in his father's stead, and use his father's authority, to do the father's business, etcetera. Adoption (placed-son) in the Bible also means that the "placed-son" understand that he/she is indeed "lord of all," through the inheritance from the Father.

When the seven thunders in **Revelation 10: 4,** as explained in **Psalm 29,** declared to **"place to the Lord sons of God,"** the Lord is saying, these sons are His, they are beloved by Him, and that they are mature enough to the "placed" as lords of all. Jesus is our pattern as to how the Father places sons.

Jesus at age twelve (12) could confound teachers (doctors). However, for about eighteen (18) years He subjected himself to His biological mother and His father by law. Paul indicated the same principle in Galatians. Before a son can be placed, the son is subjected to guardians and stewards (house-lawyers) until a certain time is fulfilled as defined by the Father.

Galatians 4:1-2: *¹Now I say that the heir,* **as long as he is a child,** *does not differ at all from a slave, though* **he is master of all,** *²but is* **under guardians and stewards until the time appointed by the father.**

Luke 2:42-49: *⁴²And when He was* **twelve years old,** *they went up to Jerusalem according to the custom of the feast. ⁴³When they had finished the days, as they returned, the Boy Jesus lingered behind in Jerusalem … 45So when they did not find Him, they returned to Jerusalem, seeking Him. ⁴⁶Now so it was that after three days they found Him in the temple, sitting in the midst of the teachers, both listening to them and asking them questions.* **⁴⁷And all who heard Him were astonished at His understanding and answers.** *⁴⁸So when they saw Him, they were amazed; and His mother said to Him, "Son, why have You done this to us? … ⁴⁹And He said to them, "Why did you seek Me? Did you not know that* **I must be about My Father's business***?" ⁵⁰But they did not understand the statement which He spoke to them.* **⁵¹Then He went down with them and came to Nazareth, and was subject to them,** *but His mother kept all these things in her heart. ⁵²And Jesus increased in wisdom and stature, and in favor with God and men.*

Paul outlined in the book to the Galatians the pattern for placing the Son and sons in general, the same pattern Jesus demonstrated. We must allow the Father to place us as sons in His season. Part of the process is we must learn **submission** to "guardians ("permitters") and stewards (house-lawyers)."

Jesus did this for eighteen years, even though He was obviously "astonishing," with His answers, teachers who were older than Him. Jesus was confirmed as the "placed" Son three times after His birth. The first time is when the Spirit descended upon Him as a dove and the Father declared that Jesus is "My beloved Son; in You I am well pleased" **(Luke 3:22).**

Luke 3:21-22: *²¹When all the people were baptized, it came to pass that Jesus also was baptized; and while He prayed, the heaven was opened.*

22And the Holy Spirit descended in bodily form like a dove upon Him, and a voice came from heaven which said, **"You are My Beloved Son; in You I am well pleased."**

Matthew 17:1-5: 1Now after six days Jesus took Peter, James, and John his brother, led them up on a high mountain by themselves; 2and **He was transfigured** *before them. His face shone like the sun, and His clothes became as white as the light. 3And behold, Moses and Elijah appeared to them, talking with Him. 4Then Peter answered and said to Jesus, "Lord, it is good for us to be here; if You wish, let us make here three tabernacles: one for You, one for Moses, and one for Elijah." 5While he was still speaking, behold, a bright cloud overshadowed them; and suddenly a voice came out of the cloud, saying,* **"This is My Beloved Son, in whom I am well pleased. Hear Him!"**

Acts 13:33: "God has fulfilled this for us their children, in that He has **raised** *up Jesus. As it is also written in the second Psalm:* **'You are My Son, Today I have begotten You.'"**

Jesus was "placed" as the Son of God when the Father publicly called Him His Beloved Son. Jesus was confirmed again as God's Beloved Son during His transfiguration in **Matthew 17.** Thirdly, the Lord Jesus was confirmed as the "placed-Son" again in His resurrection **(Acts 13:33).**

Again, our Lord Jesus is our pattern. He was placed as the Son immediately after His baptism in water by John, the Baptist. How was Jesus placed as the Son of God? The Father declared over Jesus His Sonship: *"You are my Beloved Son; in You I am well pleased."* This is when and how Jesus was "placed" as "the Son."

The pattern of Jesus is also true for us. Jesus is "the firstborn among many brothers" **(Romans 8:29).** God wants to "bring many sons to glory" **(Hebrews 2:10).**

Galatians 4:1-7: 1Now I say that the heir, as long as he is a child, does not differ at all from a slave, though he is master of all, 2but is under guardians and stewards until the **time appointed by the father.** *3Even so we, when we were children, were in bondage under the elements of the world.* **4But when the fullness of the time had come, God sent forth**

*His Son, born of a woman, born under the law, ⁵to redeem those who were under the law, **that we might receive the adoption as sons**. ⁶And because you are sons, God has sent forth the Spirit of His Son into your hearts, crying out, "Abba, Father!" ⁷Therefore you are no longer a slave **but a son**, and if a son, then an heir of God through Christ.*

According to Paul in verse **Galatians 4:7** above, the entire Church of Galatia was a corporate "son." *Therefore, **you are** no longer a slave **but a son**, and if a son, then an heir of God through Christ."* This is not a new concept, because God invented it in **Exodus 4:22-23**. It is written in **Galatians 3:26,** "For you are all sons of God through faith in Christ Jesus." "In other words of Paul, *"God sent forth His Son ... that **we might receive the 'placing' as sons."***

Allow me to relay an event to you. It was around 1988, I was in the process of reading a book on the prophetic office. As I was reading the book, I began to seek the Father again concerning my call. As I was praying the Lord began to speak to me. At that time (1988) the voice said, ***"I have not called you to be an apostle, [...], pastor, evangelist, teacher, but a [prophet]"*** (as I was hearing God speak, I blocked out some of His words and inserted. At the time, I was afraid of what God would speak contrary to what I wanted to be, a prophet).

Seventeen (17) years later, on February 6, 2005, in Maryland while by a sofa, in our home, praying, the Lord resumed His discourse with me again, with the same words He attempted to speak to me the first time in 1988. The Lord reminded me how He attempted to speak to me in 1988; and how I had blocked out His words. Amazingly, the voice of the Lord continued exactly as He spoke in 1988, ***"I have not called you to be a prophet, an apostle, an evangelist, pastor or teacher, but a son."*** In another significant conversation, I had with the Lord, the Lord also called me "my son." Those words were sweet and comforting. We are "into the praise of His glory" towards us.

Six years after the 2005 conversation with the Lord, again in the month of **"February"** 20011, I realized the depth of what the Lord was saying to me. The Lord was honoring me then in 1988 and again in 2005, and again in 2011 that the Lord was "placing me as a son" (adoption).

I did not realize until 2011 that when the Father **spoke** over Jesus, saying that Jesus is indeed His Beloved Son that the Father **spoken acknowledgement** of Jesus as His Son was the Father "placing" Jesus as the Son.[4] The goal of God the Father is to "praise" over us His voice that we are His beloved sons and that all the glory (esteem) and honor (value) that comes with Him placing us as "sons" becomes effective at that moment. Listen to the words of God through His apostolic sons.

Galatians 3:26: **For you are all sons of God** *through faith in Christ Jesus*

Galatians 4:6-7: *[6]And because you are sons, God has sent forth the* **Spirit of His Son** *into your hearts, crying out,* **"Abba, Father!"** *[7]Therefore you are no longer a slave* **but a son,** *and if a son, then an heir of God through Christ.*

Romans 8:14-16: *[14]For as many as are* **led by the Spirit of God, these are sons of God.** *[15]For you did not receive the spirit of bondage again to fear, but* **you received the Spirit of adoption (lit., placed-Son)** *by whom we cry out,* **"Abba, Father."** *[16]The Spirit Himself bears witness with our spirit that we are* **children of God.**

1 John 3:2: *Beloved,* **now we are children (lit., offspring) of God;** *and it has not yet been revealed what we shall be, but we know that when He is revealed, we shall be like Him, for we shall see Him as He is.*

John 1:12: *But as many as received Him, to them He gave the right to become* **children (lit., offspring) of God,** *to those who believe in His name:*

---

[4] As taught by Dr. Kelley Varner

Hebrews 2:10: *For it was fitting for Him, for whom are all things and by whom are all things,* **in bringing many sons to glory**, *to make the captain of their salvation perfect through sufferings.*

Ephesians 1:4-5: [4] *... He chose us in Him before the foundation of the world, that we should be holy and without blame before Him in love,* [5]*having* **predestined** *us to* **adoption as sons (lit., placing as sons)** *by Jesus Christ to Himself, according to the good pleasure of His will*

"Predestined" is also defined as "pre-defined." God **"pre-definition"** of us is to become His sons of glory in the earth. This destiny to be **"placed as sons"** is only fulfilled by/through Jesus Christ, Himself. He came that we may be delivered form the control of the elements of the world.

He came to show us that we are "lord or master of all" as sons of God, through Christ. What an honor, what glory the Father has given us. He has given us the better (lit., different") name by placing us as sons.

Hebrews 1:4-5: [4]*Having become so much better than the angels, as He has by inheritance obtained* **a more excellent name (lit., different name)** *than they.* [5]*For to which of the angels did He ever say:* **"You are My Son;** *Today I have begotten You"? And again: "I will be* **to (lit., into)** *Him* **a Father,** *And He shall be* **to (lit., into)** *Me a* **Son"?**

The name "Son" is **"different"** from the name "angels." Angels submit to the Son; and they worship the Son. Angels minister "through" those (His sons) who are heirs of salvation. Jesus did not take on the nature of angels; He took on the "Seed" of Abraham. And the promise to Abraham is "sure to **all** the seed" **(Romans 4:13 w/4:16).**

Hebrews 2:16-17: [16]*For indeed He does not give aid to angels, but He does give aid to the* **seed** *of Abraham.* [17]*Therefore, in all things He had to be* **made like His brethren**

Galatians 3:26; 29: [26]*For you are* **all sons of God through faith in Christ Jesus** *...*[29]*And if* **you are Christ's,** *then you are* **Abraham's seed,** *and heirs according to* **the promise**

Romans 4:13-16: [13]For ***the promise*** *that he would be the **heir of the world*** *was not to Abraham or to his **seed** through the law, but through the righteousness of faith …* [16]*Therefore it is of faith that it might be according to grace, **so that the promise might be sure to all the seed**, not only to those who are of the law, but also to those who are of the faith of Abraham, who is the father of us all.*

The Spirit of the "Placed-Son"

Romans 8:14-16: *14For as many as are led by the Spirit of God, these are sons of God. 15For you did not receive the spirit of bondage again to fear,* **but you received the Spirit of adoption** *by whom we cry out, "Abba, Father." 16***The Spirit Himself** *bears witness with* **our spirit** *that we are children of God*

There are many who go about calling themselves "sons;" and I am not so sure that they all are sons. That is, their spirit does not confess that Jesus is their Lord and King. Therefore, I thought it fit to take some time to show that sonship with "the Father of spirits" is linked to "our spirit" **confessing** Jesus Christ. If our spirit is not confessing Jesus, then we are not sons of God. The truth is that sonship begins with **"the Spirit** of 'placed-son;'" and it consummate in our bodies being placed as sons (sons of resurrection) — **Romans 8:23, Luke 20:36.**

If we have "received the Spirit of 'placed-son';" then our spirit will "**cry** Abba Father." Paul also said that it is "the Spirit Himself" that "bears witness with **our spirit** that we are the 'offspring' of God." "Our spirit" is linked to sonship (being placed as a son).

Galatians 4:4-6: *4But when the fullness of the time had come, God sent forth His Son, born of a woman, born under the law, 5to redeem those who were under the law, that we* **might receive the adoption as sons.** *6And* **because** *you are* **sons,** *God has sent forth* **the Spirit** *of His Son into your* **hearts,** *crying out, "Abba, Father!"*

Again, Paul linked being adopted (placed as sons) is by "the Spirit of His Son" (Jesus) being sent out into our **hearts.** According to **1 Peter 3:4,** our spirit is the "hidden man of the **heart.**" Again, if we are the Fathers sons, then we should be crying, "Abba Father." The spirit of a legitimate and genuine son will cry Abba Father. This means that the spirit of a legitimate son will say all things are possible with the Father. This is what "the Son of God" prayed on His way to be crucified.

*Mark 14:36: And He said, **"Abba, Father, all things are possible for You***. Take this cup away from Me; nevertheless, not what I will, but what You will."*

The verse above shows the Spirit of Jesus (the Spirit of Sonship) crying out to the Father, "All things are possible." The spirits of God's other sons should do the same. We cry "Abba, Father, all things are possible for you." The Spirit bears witness with our spirit that we are the sons of God. Our spirits must say that Jesus has come in the flesh for us to be considered true sons.

*1 John 4:1-3: [1]Beloved, do not believe every spirit, but test the spirits, whether they are of God, because many false prophets have gone out into the world. [2]**By this you know the Spirit of God: Every spirit that confesses that Jesus Christ has come in the flesh is of God,** [3]**and every spirit that does not confess that Jesus Christ has come in the flesh is not of God.** And this is the spirit of the Antichrist, which you have heard was coming, and is now already in the world.*

In the verses above what makes a person/prophet true, is when their **"spirit … confesses** that Jesus Christ has come in the flesh." Conversely, in the verses above what makes a person false, is when their "spirit … does **not** confess that Jesus Christ has come in the flesh." This is strong and must be taken seriously. What makes a person false, especially a worldly prophet, is the "spirit's confession."

Most are caught up with confessing with their mouths **(Romans 10:9).** Yet, confession with the mouth is but the beginning of confession or one only facet of confessing. One's **spirit** must also **confess (lit., say (the) same word) that** Jesus Christ has come in the flesh. And **1 John 4:1-2** says if a person spirit **does not** confess that Jesus Christ has come in the flesh that person is "not 'out of' God." Our spirits must confess that Jesus came in the flesh 2000 years ago; and our spirit must also confess that Jesus has come **in our flesh,** after we fulfill **Romans 10:9,** by first confessing with our mouth and believing with our hearts.

Our spirits must confess ("say the same") as our mouths' confess. Some saints get deceived, a lot, by fake sons/daughters who confess with their mouth, but their spirits do not confess Jesus has come in their flesh and that He came in the flesh 2000 years ago. "The Spirit bears witness with our spirits that we are the offspring of God."

Our "spirits" must "confess that Jesus Christ has come in the flesh" (which includes our spirits confessing that Jesus also has come in **our** flesh). According to Jesus there is a "sound" that "spirit" makes, and part of that sound is our spirit confessing (saying the same) that Jesus Christ came in the flesh 2000 years ago. And, He has also come in the flesh of those who have His Spirit.

John 3:6; 8: ⁶*"That which is born of the flesh is flesh, and **that which is born of the Spirit is spirit**...' * ⁸*"**The wind (lit., spirit)** blows where it wishes, and you **hear the sound** of it, but cannot tell where it comes from and where it goes. **So is everyone who is born of the Spirit."***

We just read "that which ('everyone who') is born of the **Spirit is spirit."** Thus, once we are born from above, we are spirit. "He that is joined (keep company) with the Lord is **one spirit** with the Lord **(1 Corinthians 6:17).** According to Jesus, spirit also makes **"sound."**

Jesus said that we can "hear the sound" of "the 'spirit' blowing." One of the sounds that the spirit makes is the word of **confession** that Jesus has come in the flesh. Our spirit must **"confess" (lit., say (the) same word)** that Jesus has come in the flesh 2000 years ago, literally and He has come in us by the infilling of His Holy Spirit.

I know that this is strong; and it should make a person examine themselves to make sure their spirit is confessing Jesus Christ. Falsehood springs out of spirits that are illegitimate. Thus, some are spurious sons/daughters when their spirits do not confess that same thing their mouth is saying. Our spirit confession must match our mouth confession.

If those who claim to be sons/daughters of God spirits are confessing an illegitimate sound; then these sons/daughters are not from **"the Father of spirits"** as they claim. According to **1 John 4,** spirits that do not confess Jesus are false. The book of Hebrews calls them "illegitimate and not sons."

*Hebrews 12:7-9: ⁷If you endure chastening, God deals with you as with sons; for what son is there whom a father does not chasten? ⁸But if you are without chastening, of which all have become partakers, then you are **illegitimate and not sons**. ⁹Furthermore, we have had **human fathers** who corrected us, and we paid them respect. Shall we not much more readily be in subjection to the **Father of spirits** and live?*

Human fathers chasten us in the flesh. "The Father of **spirits**" chastens us in our spirits, which can affect our flesh and Joints **(Hebrews 12:8; 11-13).** If our spirits cannot endure the Father's chastening then we **"are illegitimate and not sons."** This is another witness that tells us that it is our spirits that makes us sons.

If a person cannot be corrected in his/her spirit by the Father of our spirits; and if a person cannot be corrected by those under the authority of the Father, then a person without corrections is not a true son/daughter. According to the text above a spirit that cannot be corrected is illegitimate and not sons. If one becomes illegitimate, then the confession of his/her spirit is not of God.

"Illegitimate" literally means "spurious," "bastards" and "not from the claim" (see Strong's). Jesus considered the Pharisees as illegitimate. The Pharisees were "not from the claimed" **(John 8:41).** They "claimed" to be born of God. But Jesus said they were of the Devil **(John 8:38; 44).** Why? According to the writer of Hebrews, they could not be corrected; and thus, had a wrong spirit. Their spirit did not confess Jesus. The Pharisees refused to acknowledge Jesus as the Christ, the Son of the living God **(see John 9:22).**

Psalm 51:10: Create in me a clean heart, O God, and renew a steadfast (upright) spirit within me.

*1 Peter 3:4, KJV: But let it be **the hidden man of the heart**, in that which is not corruptible, even the ornament **of a meek and quiet spirit**, which is in the sight of God of great price.*

When David confessed his combined sin of adultery and murder, he went straight to the place where he needed correction—the hidden man of his heart—where his spirit dwelled. Because of what David did, he knew his heart was dirty and his "spirit" was crooked. Thus, his cry, "Create in me a **clean** heart, O God, and renew an **'upright' spirit** within me."

The spirit of David is what makes him a son of God. Thus, he wanted his spirit to be corrected to uprightness again. Why? It is the spirit confession that is important. David "declared" boldly that he was a "son" by God in **Psalms 2:7.** Therefore, David had the Spirit of the Son in him.

We are sons, if the Spirit bears witness with our spirits that we are the offspring of God. We are sons of the Spirit of God if our spirits also confess that Jesus Christ is come in the flesh. We are <u>legitimate</u> sons, if we allow the Father of spirits to correct our spirits; and **the Father of spirits corrects our spirits by correcting the way we think.** We must change our mindset into believing that we are indeed sons to the Holy Father.

*Ephesians 4:23: And be renewed in the **spirit of your mind***

*2 Timothy 1:7: For God has not given us a **spirit** of fear, but of power and of love and of **a sound mind (lit. saved mental disposition).***

Paul said that God did not give us "a spirit of fear." Then, the question must be asked what Spirit did the Father give us? God has … given us … **a spirit … of power.** God has … given us … **a spirit … of love.** God has … given us … a **spirit … of a "saved mind."** Thus, we do have a **spirit of a "saved mind"** if we have the Spirit of the Son in us. Paul echoed this again in Ephesians. He said, "be renewed in the **spirit of your mind.**"

There is a spirit of your mind. The Bible does <u>not</u> say there is a soul of your mind. Nor does it say that your mind is in your soul. Yes, our soul is linked to our desires expressed through our minds to appreciate the earthly realm. But your mind is linked to your spirit. Thus, when the Father of spirits corrects our spirits, He is also correcting our minds.

*Romans 8:6: For to be **carnally minded** is death, but to be **spiritually minded** is life and peace.*

The verse above **literally reads: "For the disposition of the flesh is death; yet the disposition of the spirit is life and peace."** The Father has to correct the disposition of our minds. He does not want our minds on fleshly things. The Father wants our minds on "Spirit" — sonship.

We must be renewed in the spirit of our minds. Our spirits have to be corrected by the Father of spirits to walk in the "disposition of a saved mind." Our spirit must confess Jesus Christ is come in our flesh. Our spirits are to display all the glory of sonship in the Beloved, Jesus.

Remember, if you have received the Holy Spirit then ***"you received the Spirit of 'placed-son' by whom we cry out, "Abba, Father." The Spirit Himself** bears witness with **our spirit** that we are children of God" **(Romans 8:15-16).** And *"By this you **know the Spirit of God:** Every **spirit** that **confesses** that **Jesus Christ** has **come in the flesh** is of God"* **(I John 4:2).** *"And **because** you are **sons,** God has sent forth **the Spirit** of His Son into your **hearts,** crying out, "Abba, Father"* **(Galatians 4:6)***!* Amen! So be it!

The 7th Angel, the Interruption

*Revelation 10:5-7: ⁵The angel whom I saw standing on the sea and on the land raised up his hand to heaven ⁶and swore by Him who lives forever and ever, who created heaven and the things that are in it, the earth and the things that are in it, and the sea and the things that are in it, that there should be **delay no longer (lit., uninterrupted time (chronos) no longer),** ⁷but in **the days of the sounding of the seventh angel,** when he is about to sound, **the mystery of God would be finished,** as He declared to His servants the prophets.*

In the reference above we see that "chronos" (uninterrupted time) would not continue as is. The Mighty Angel indicated the two (2) things or one (1) thing, depending on how you read the Greek text, which would interrupt time. The interruption of chronos is done by "the days of the sounding of the seventh angel," and/or "the mystery of God is finished." Here are some variations of how the Greek texts for **Revelation 10:7** are translated.

*Revelation 10:7, **Young's Literal Translation**: But in the days of the voice of the seventh messenger, when he may be about to sound, **and** the secret of God may be finished, as He did declare to His own servants, to the prophets.*

*Revelation 10:7, **ASV**: But in the days of the voice of the seventh angel, when he is about to sound, **then** is finished the mystery of God, according to the good tidings which he declared to his servants the prophets.*

*Revelation 10:7, **CLV (Concordant Literal New Testament)**: But in the days of the seventh messenger's voice, whenever he may be about to be trumpeting, the secret of God is consummated **also,** as He evangelizes to His own slaves and the prophets.*

Here is how **Revelation 10:7** in the "Interlinear Scripture Analyzer [Basic]" reads (parenthesis and bold text added by this author): *"But in the days of-the sound of-the seventh messenger when-ever he-may-be-being-about to-be-trumpeting **and** is-finished the close-keep (mystery) of the God as He-well-messaged the of-self slaves the before-avers (prophets)."*

Based on the references, if we look at **Revelation 10:7** as two events that interrupt time (chronos), then the days of the seventh angel, whenever he is about to sound, is an interruption of time; and the mystery of God being finished is also a possible second event that interrupts time (chronos). Yet as we will see both these events can be counted as one (1); because both are linked to God placing mature sons in the earth to bring the Father glory.

In this chapter, we will look at the "interruption by the seventh angel;" and we will look at the mystery of God being finished in another chapter. An understanding of the **interruption** that the seventh angel enacted will give an appreciation for the rest of the things that encompasses the mystery of God being finished.

In the days of the voice of the seventh angel, the Lord will interrupt time by commissioning His mature sons. The mature sons of God will no longer be governed by the elements of the world, but will interrupt time with power and glory, like Jesus interrupted "chronos" by manifesting His glory.

According to **Revelation 10:6,** cited above, there will be "**delay** no longer." The Greek literally read, "**'Uninterrupted time' not still shall be."** Per **Revelation 10:7,** the seventh angel "and," "or" the mystery of God being finished will cause an interruption of "chronos" time. God is going to insert His sons and daughters of glory into time and interrupt the elements (arrangement in a series) of the world as we know it. We will see in a moment this same pattern in "the Son" — Jesus.

Revelation 10:7 also states that chronos (uninterrupted duration) will be interrupted in "the **days** of the sounding of the seventh angel." When the seventh angel sounds his trumpet, it will be sounding for **"days."** Thus, whoever this "messenger" is and how ever he delivers his message, his "sounding" or his "voice" will interrupt the normalcy of time for "days."

Jesus is the pattern for the "interruption of time;" and according to Jesus' pattern, time being interrupted is the Father, placing Jesus as the mature Son in the earth, in love delivering those oppressed of the Devil. Thus, the seventh angel interrupted time because he represents **"placed" mature sons** who are trumpeting mature messages and living a mature lifestyle (imaging Jesus[5]) by bringing glory to the Father who "placed" them (through faith, knowledge, character, and power of Jesus).

Galatians 4:1-5: *¹Now I say that the heir,* **as long as (lit., upon as uninterrupted time)** *he is a child, does not differ at all from a slave, though he is master of all, ²but is under guardians and stewards until the* **time appointed (lit., preplaced)** *by the father. ³Even so we, when we were children, were in bondage under the elements of the world. ⁴But when* **the fullness of the time (lit., the filling of the uninterrupted time)** *had come, God sent forth His Son, born of a woman, born under the law, ⁵to redeem those who were under the law, that we might receive* **the adoption as sons (lit., the placing as sons).**

The Mighty Angel, Jesus, declared that **"'uninterrupted time' would be no longer, but in the days of-the sound of-the seventh angel when-ever he-is-about to-be-trumpeting;" the elemental trajectory of the earth and the sea would be interrupted unto salvation.** Thus, it is the seventh angel that brings about an interruption to time before he even sounds his trumpet. In other words, it was not the trumpet sound that interrupted time, initially. What interrupted time initially is the fact that the seventh angel **"is about to sound"[6]** his trumpet; and he cannot "be about to sound" until he is "prepared inwardly" to maturity, and then placed as a trumpeter by the Father.

Saying it another way, the reason it was the angel that interrupted time is because of his maturity as **a** son of God and the fact that the Father "placed" him as a mature son after the seventh angel prepared himself, inwardly. "So, the seven angels who had the seven trumpets **prepared**[7] themselves to sound" **(Revelation 8:6).** Jesus followed the same pattern as outlined in **Galatians 4:1-2.**

---

[5] Romans 8:29
[6] Or, impending to sound
[7] Greek: Hetoimazo ("internal fitness" according to Strong's Concordance)

Galatians 4:1-5: *¹Now I say that the heir,* **as long as (lit., upon as uninterrupted time)** *he is a child, does not differ at all from a slave, though he is master of all,* *²but is under guardians and stewards until the* **time appointed (lit., preplaced, purposed)** *by the father.* *³Even so we, when we were children, were in bondage under the elements of the world.* *⁴But when* **the fullness of the time (lit., the filling of the uninterrupted time)** *had come, God sent forth His Son, born of a woman, born under the law,* *⁵to redeem those who were under the law, that we might receive* **the adoption as sons (lit., the placing as sons).**

In the verses above, we see that a "child" can be "master (lord) of all;" yet that "child" is no different from a slave … until **the filling of uninterrupted time,** preplaced by the Father. Thus, uninterrupted time is linked to immaturity. In addition, **Galatians 4:4** said when the "filling of uninterrupted time had come, God sent forth His Son." Thus, the Son, Jesus, interrupted time when the Father placed Him in the earth as the Son (Jesus was born as a child but was given as the Son[8]). A mature son interrupts time. An immature son is controlled by the cycle of time.

Jesus was placed as the mature Son in the "filling of chronos (time)." Jesus was under "guardians and stewards until the "uninterrupted time" was filled. But when Jesus was "placed," as the Son of God at His baptism in water, as the Father declared that "This is My Beloved Son, in whom I am well pleased;" Jesus was no longer under "guardians (permitters) and stewards (house-lawyers)." All the "elements of the world" is subjected to Jesus. The Son is free; and the sons placed by God, the Father are free!

Jesus, as the mature Son dominated the elements of the world. Jesus the mature son interrupted time in the filling of time. The same is true for the seventh angel. The seventh angel will be placed as a son (a corporate son), by the mature Son, Jesus the Mighty Messenger who declared that "there will no longer be 'uninterrupted time,' but in the days of the voice of the seventh angel …."

---

[8] Isaiah 9:6

In **Galatians 4,** we learned that time was interrupted by Jesus, the Son of God. Paul also stated that we were also children, "in **'slavery'** under the elements of the world. But when the fullness of the time had come, God sent forth His Son … that we might receive the adoption as sons (lit., the placing as sons)."

The seventh angel had authority to interrupt time; because the seventh angel represents mature sons who now dominated the elements of the world, which includes "times." The seventh angel was placed as a mature son, before he trumpeted, because the trumpeter's message must also be demonstrated by the trumpeter. The seventh angel or the seventh trumpet declared that "the kingdoms of this **world** became of our Lords and of His Christ" **(Revelation 11:15).**

The mature Son is no longer "in **'slavery'** under the elements of the **world" (Galatians 4:3).** Sons are not to walk in slavery to sin or under sin![9] It follows that the matured seventh angel trumpet resulted in conquest or conversion of the **"world"** (the kingdom of the world became our Lord and His Christ, which also fulfills a promise to Abraham and his seed — see **Romans 4:13).** "Time (chronos)," an element of the world, will be interrupted again. Jesus did it; and a group of mature messengers will interrupt time again.

*Galatians 4:3-4:[3]Even so we, when we were children, were in 'slavery' under the **elements of the world**. [4]But when **the fullness of the time** (lit., **the filling of the uninterrupted time**) had come, God sent forth His Son … **born under the law**.*

*Galatians 4:9-11: [9]But now after you have known God, or rather are known by God, how is it that you turn again to the weak and beggarly **elements**, to which you desire again to be in bondage? [10]You observe **days** and **months** and **seasons** and **years**. [11]I am afraid for you, lest I have labored for you in vain.*

---

[9] John 8:31-36; Galatians 4:1;6-7

"Elements of the world" are linked to "days" (a form of time), "months" (a form of time), "seasons" (a form of time), "years" (a form of time), and "law" (a set period of approximately 1500 years from Moses to Jesus's establishment of the New Covenant). Jesus, as the mature "placed" Son conquered the elements of the world. Jesus interrupted time. Jesus interrupted the religious laws of the Jews. Jesus interrupted the cycle of death. Time is death. God said to Adam, "In the **day** that you eat of it you shall **surely die**" **(Genesis 2:17).**

Thus, time ("in the day") is linked to "dying by death." Jesus destroyed the time of death. Jesus laid down His life when He wanted to; and Jesus picked up His life in three days by the authority of the Father **(John 10:17).** No one could take Jesus' life at their will **(John 10:18).** Jesus interrupted their chronos! So likewise, the seventh angel and the two witnesses shall interrupt time.

The system (the world) shall be made subject to God mature messengers! Time and death shall be made subject to the Father's mature sons. Jesus' enemy could not take Him because His "hour had not yet come" **(John 7:30).** The same is true for the two witnesses. The beast could not kill them until their days (1260 days) were completed **(Revelation 11:7).**

In addition, the seven angels were given seven trumpets **(Revelation 8:2).** The seven angels also "prepared" (lit., prepared internally) to sound **(Revelation 8:6).** Per an interpretation of **Revelation 8**, their preparation can take from seven and a half (7 ½) years to twenty-one (21) years. That is, the half an hour in Revelation 8:1 may be symbolic of approximately, seven and a half (7.5) years or twenty-one (~21) years.

Internal preparation for the Lord's ministry is of utmost importance; and thus, I will take some time to show you a "time" principle related to preparation time. Jesus prepared Himself to sound His trumpet; and we must also prepare ourselves as sons to also sound the trumpets. Here is the mathematics that show this principle using the apostle Peter's thousand years/one day principle as seen in **2 Peter 3:8, or** the year day principle used in **Numbers 14:34.**

Numbers 14:34: 1 day equal 1 year; thus 360 days divided by 24 hours equals 15 years, which equates to 1 hour; and it follow that a half an hour would be 7 ½ years. Thus, preparation to sound off prophetically, can take up to 7 ½ years of preparation for some.

2 Peter 3:8: 1,000 years divided by 24 hours equals 41.67 years/hour. That is 41.67 years equals one (1) hour per apostle Peter's principle; hence a ½ of one (1) hour is approximately twenty-one years (~42 years ÷2=~21 years). This may seem like a long time to prepare; especially with the zealousness of young ministers today ascending into ministry before they are fully "internally-prepared."

Jesus internally-prepared the original disciples twenty-four/seven for approximately three and a half years (3 ½ years).[10] Therefore, twenty-four (24) hours multiplied by three hundred-sixty (360) days/year equals eight thousand six hundred-forty (8,640) hours, multiplied by three and a half (3 ½) years equals thirty thousand two hundred and forty (30,240) hours. Yes, the original disciples may have invested approximately 30,240 hours in preparation with Jesus, before Jesus ascended to the right hand of God.

With that said, comparing the zealousness of most young ministers today, most seems to fall short of internal-preparation. Allow me to explain. Let's be liberal and say that most ministers/saints of today give Jesus about two (2) hours per day, multiplied by three hundred-sixty (360) days/years, equals seven hundred and twenty (720) hours, then multiplied by three and a half (3 ½) years, equals two thousand five hundred twenty (2,520) hours. In other word, the original disciples of Jesus probably invested twelve (12) times as many hours in three and a half years with Jesus than the

---

[10] Dr. Stephen Everett

ministers of today, according to my hypothetical estimate (30,240 hours ÷ 2,520 hours=12).

This means, it could take the young ministers of today twelves times as long with Jesus and His Holy Spirit to be prepared like the original apostles of the Lamb. That is, it would take approximately forty-two (42) years to equal the hours the disciples accomplished in three and a half (3 ½) years with Jesus. Thus, the approximate time of twenty-one (21) years of internal-preparation seems appropriate. Jesus prepared Himself for eighteen (18) years, Moses prepared himself for forty (40) years, David and Joseph may have gone through thirteen (13) to seventeen (17) years of preparation before rulership. Did Paul prepare for three (3) to fourteen (14) years, as implied in **Galatians 1:8** and **Galatians 2:1**)?

With regards to the seventh angel, he was declared eligible, after-internal preparation) to interrupt time. Not only was he given a trumpet (prophetic voice), not only did he prepare himself inwardly; he was given authority to interrupt time. *"And I saw another mighty angel ... cried ... that there should be time no longer: But in the days of the voice of the seventh angel, when he shall begin to sound..." (Revelation 10:1-7a).*

The Mystery of God is Finished

Revelation 10:6-7: *[6]And swore by Him who lives forever and ever, who created heaven and the things that are in it, the earth and the things that are in it, and the sea and the things that are in it, **that there should be delay no longer,** [7]but in the days of the sounding of the seventh angel, when he is about to sound, **the mystery of God would be finished,** as He declared to His servants the prophets.*

There will also be "days" when time will be interrupted as the "mystery of God" (Christ in us and the Father in Christ) is finished or matured. There will be "days" when the seventh trumpet will sound; and the kingdoms of this world will become our Lords and His Christ; and there will be "days" when the mystery of God is completed in us, which subdues the worldly elements. This completion of the mystery of God also interrupts time, as we will see. However, first we must begin by defining the "mystery of God."

Colossians 2:1-2: *[1]For I want you to know what a great conflict I have for you and those in Laodicea, and for as many as have not seen my face in the flesh, [2]that their hearts may be encouraged, being knit together in love, and attaining to all riches of the full assurance of understanding, to the knowledge of **the mystery of God, both of the Father and of Christ***

The phrase **"the mystery of God"** is defined as **"both (or even) the father and of Christ."** The Majority texts reads **"the mystery of-the God and Father and of-the Christ."** This statement of truth is one of the most beautiful truths of the Bible. This mystery of God (of the Father and of Christ) is what our Lord Jesus prayed about before He was crucified, buried, and resurrected. His goal for us is for this mystery of God to be fulfilled in us. The mystery of God is this, Christ in us, and the Father in Christ, He in us and the Father in Him, that Christ and His Church may be one, even as the Father and Christ is one.

John 17:20-23: ²⁰*"I do not pray for these alone, but also for those who will believe in Me through their word;* ²¹*"that they all may be one, as You, Father, are in Me, and I in You; that they also may be one in Us, that the world may believe that You sent Me.* ²²*"And the glory which You gave Me I have given them, that they may be one just as We are one:* ²³*"I in them, and You in Me; that they may be made perfect in one, and that the world may know that You have sent Me, and have loved them as You have loved Me."*

Colossians 1:27: *To them **God willed** to make known what are the riches of **the glory of this mystery** among the Gentiles: which is **Christ in you, the hope of glory.***

When Jesus was revealed, He declared God as the Father; and the Father glorified Jesus to be His Son. The mystery of God is **Christ in us,** and the **Father in Christ**. That is, the place of maturity is to realize that we are one with Christ, Jesus, because He is in us. This is because Christ, Jesus is one with the Father; because the Father is in Him, and He is in the Father. The Lord Jesus, Himself said, "That they all may be **one, as You, Father, are in Me**, and **I in You;** that **they also may be one in Us."**

Time will be interrupted when "oneness" between the Church and the Lord Jesus is realized. That is, we realize that the Christ is in us, and we are in the Father, through Jesus. The "world" will be interrupted (becoming our Lord's and His Christ) when the Church of our Lord Jesus Christ realizes her oneness with Jesus. **"I (Jesus) in them,** and **You (Father) in Me;** that they may be made **'mature' in one,** and **that the world may know that You have sent Me.**

The mystery of God being finished will interrupt time as we know it. The mystery of God being finished will interrupt the elements of time in the world as we know "times" to be. Once the mystery of God is finished (completed, matured), the world will come to know that the Father sent the Son (Jesus Christ) to save the world.

The world will become the kingdom of our Lord without manmade weapons. The kingdoms of the world will be translated as we were translated into God's kingdom **(Hebrews 12:27-28 w/Colossians 1:13).** The Father of glory will bring many sons to glory. "And the **glory** which You gave Me I have given them, that they may be one just as We are one" **(John 17:22).**

There is a glory that the Father has for each of His sons and daughters that will interrupt the natural course of things. Christ in us the hope of glory; the glory of oneness with the Father; a glory that rules the elements of the world. This glory also includes the love the Father has in us; that is, the same love the Father has for Jesus is the same love the Father has for us and in us.

John 17:22-23, KJV: *²²And **the glory** which you gave me I have given them; that they may be one, even as we are one:* *²³I in them, and you in me, that they may be made perfect in one; and that **the world** may know that you have **sent me, and have loved them, as thou hast loved me**.*

Colossians 1:27: *To them God willed to make known what are the riches of **the glory of this mystery** among the Gentiles: which is **Christ in you, the hope of glory.***

There is a glory of the mystery of God. This glory is realizing that the glory of Christ being the Son of God is also "in us." The glory of knowing the God loves us the same way He loved Jesus. What truth! We are loved equally as Jesus Christ, through the sacrifice of Christ. This glory of Jesus in us and the Father in Jesus and the love of God in us interrupts the natural course of the world, because Jesus is then seen in us by the world.

John 2:1-11: *¹On the third day there was a wedding in Cana of Galilee, and the mother of Jesus was there. ²Now both Jesus and His disciples were invited to the wedding. ³And when they ran out of wine, the mother of Jesus said to Him, "They have no wine." ⁴Jesus said to her, "Woman, what does your concern have to do with Me? My hour has not yet come." ⁵His mother said to the servants, "Whatever He says to you, do it." ⁶Now there were set there six waterpots of stone, according to the manner of purification of the Jews, containing twenty or thirty gallons apiece. ⁷Jesus said to them, "Fill the waterpots with water." And they filled them up to the brim. ⁸And He said to them, "Draw some out now, and take it to the master of the feast." And they took it.* ⁹*When the master of the feast had tasted the water that was made wine and did not know where it came from (but the servants who had drawn the water knew), the master of the feast called the bridegroom.* ¹⁰*And he said to him, "Every man at the beginning sets out the good wine, and when the guests have well drunk, then the inferior. You have kept the good wine until now!"* ¹¹*This beginning of signs Jesus did in Cana of Galilee and **manifested His glory;** and His disciples believed in Him.*

Jesus manifested His glory at will. How was this possible? Jesus and the Father is one. The Scripture said that the God would be "into" Jesus as the Father and Jesus would be "into" the Father as the "Son." Thus, as Jesus declared, the Father is He who does the work through Jesus, the Son. The mystery of God being matured involves the glory of sonship being manifested at His will mixed with our wills to interrupt the natural course of things, through His love.

At the wedding that Jesus, His mother, and His disciples attended; Jesus interrupted the elements by changing water to wine! He could do this because God was into Him the Father and He was into God the Son. Thus, the glory that God gave Him could be manifested.

Hebrews 1:4-5: ⁴*Having become so much better than the angels, as He has by inheritance obtained a more excellent name than they.* ⁵*For to which of the angels did He ever say: "You are My Son; Today I have begotten You"? And again: "I will be **to (Greek "eis," into)** Him a Father, And He shall be **to (Greek "eis," into)** Me a Son"?*

2 Peter 1:17: *For He received from God the Father **honor** and **glory** when such a voice came to Him from the **Excellent Glory:** "This is **My Beloved Son,** in whom I am well pleased."*

John 17:22-23a: ²²*And **the glory** which You gave Me I have given them, that they may be one just as We are one:* ²³ ***"I in them, and You in Me ...."***

John 2:9-11: ⁹*... **the water that was made wine** ...* ¹¹*This beginning of signs **Jesus** did in Cana of Galilee and **manifested His glory....***

The glory of Jesus was that He is the "sent" Beloved Son. True sonship is when the Father is into His children and the children are into the Father, because of His love for us and into us. In the natural, a true father should father his children to the point that he is "into" them (his love impression is in them); and the children must also be into their father (into their father's love for them and thus declares the Father). This is the glory of the **oneness** of the "mystery of God, both the Father and of Christ."

The Father is "into" Jesus; and Jesus is "into" the Father. The Father was so "into" Jesus that Jesus declared that *"he who has seen [Jesus] has seen the Father" (John 14:9);* and Jesus was so into the Father that He also said: *"Do you not believe that I am in the Father, and the Father in Me?* **The words that I speak to you I do not speak on My own authority; but the Father who dwells in Me does the works.** *Believe Me that I am in the Father and the Father in Me, or else believe Me for the sake of the works themselves" (John 14:10-11).*

There is a glory of sonship that God, the Father has for us. It is only for those who mature into "the unity (lit., oneness) of the faith … of the Son of God;" and into "the unity (lit., oneness) … of the 'exact knowledge' of the Son of God." Christ in us is the expectation of glory. And just as our Lord Jesus manifested His glory by interrupting the element of water, the Church will interrupt time in the days of the seventh angel.

John 2:9-11: [9]*… **the water that was made wine** … [11]This beginning of signs **Jesus** did in Cana of Galilee and **manifested His glory**….*

*1 Corinthians 2:7: But we speak the wisdom of God in a mystery, the hidden wisdom which God ordained before the ages **for our glory**.*

*1 Corinthians 2:9: But as it is written: "Eye has not seen, nor ear heard, nor have entered into the heart of man the **things which God has prepared** for those who love Him."*

According to **1 Corinthians 2:7,** there is some "wisdom of God in a mystery which God 'predefined' for our glory." Yes, a mystery of wisdom for "our glory" The Father "predefined" that our Lord

Jesus would know the wisdom that water can be turned to wine to Jesus' glory! There is a glory for you that no man has seen, nor heard. The Father alone will reveal these things to His sons of glory.

No one ever saw water turned to wine before Jesus did it. No one has ever raised a man that was dead for four days come back to life, except Jesus who raised Lazarus from the dead. The same is true in the days of the seventh angel; things that we have not seen or heard will be manifested for our glory, so that the Son and the Father can be glorified! Jesus did this regularly; He manifested glory that can only come from God; glory that was never seen before.

When Jesus healed the blind man, the now "seeing" man declared *"Since the world (lit., age) began it has been unheard of that anyone opened the eyes of one who was born blind" (John 9:32).* Jesus did some things that were never done before He came; and the Father has reserved some "glory" for us too. I will cite a few of the many "glory" the Lord Jesus has manifested through us.

In the early 1990s, while living in North Carolina, a sister came to me with her daughter. Her daughter's hair was patchy, falling out and noticeably short. When I saw them, I felt deep compassion for them. The mother asked me to pray for her daughter. I laid my hands on her hair and head and prayed. About thirty (30) days later, the lady returned with her daughter showing me and Judith the result of the prayer.

The Lord caused the young girl's hair ("her glory") to re-grow down to the middle of her back. When, they came by I could not grasp how quickly her hair had regrown, not just an inch or two; but her hair had grown reaching the middle of her back. They were so happy and appreciative for what the Lord had supernaturally done for them. This is a manifestation of glory that the Lord wants to show through His Church.

Another time, during the early 2000s, my wife (Judith) went to speak at a Church in Baltimore, MD. After the message, she began to pray for those who desired prayer. There was a sister who came up for prayer. My wife prayed for her, and the lady was healed from drugs, permanently. Judith's account though was interesting. My wife said that she saw Jesus walk out of her (my wife's) body, laid hands on the lady and then Jesus went back into her (my wife's) body. Again, this lady never went back to abusing drugs; and she is currently doing the work of the ministry. This is a manifestation of glory that the Lord wants to show through His Church.

Another time, around 1987, I accompanied a pastor to visit a woman in a crazy home in Jacksonville, NC. She asked us to pray. The pastor and I laid our hands on the lady and prayed. As I prayed I physically felt virtue (ability of God's power) leaving my hand and going into this woman. When we got finished praying, the lady turned to me and said, "When you prayed for me I felt virtue leave you and enter my body." About two (2) weeks later she was released from the crazy home; and she came to Church. Again, this is a manifestation of glory that the Lord wants to show through His Church.

During the early 2000s, my wife and I were invited to preach in Pennsylvania at Apostle Earl Palmer. On this day, Judith was finishing praying for the ladies; however, as Judith continued praying, I witnessed a lady sitting. I could see that she had been subjected to a walking cane with bandages on her foot. As Judith continued to pray, the Holy Spirit healed the woman. She leaped up and began to jump around saying "I am healed," "I am healed" as she began to thank God, running and holding other sisters telling them what had just happened to her. She was so elated about her supernatural healing. This is a manifestation of glory that the Lord wants to show through His Church.

During the days of the seventh trumpet, glory that was once unseen and unheard of will be displayed as the mystery of God "reaches its desired goal." Time as we know will be interrupted. The elements of the world will be interrupted by the Church of Jesus Christ. The mystery of God will be finished. The Father will bring to completion the expectation that we are **one** with Christ Jesus and Jesus Christ is one with the Father. Jesus in us, and the Father in Jesus that the world may know that the Father sent Jesus; and that the world may know that the Father loves us as He loved Jesus! So be it!

The Days of the 7ᵗʰ Angel

Revelation 10:5-7: *⁵The angel whom I saw standing on the sea and on the land raised up his hand to heaven ⁶and* ***swore*** *by Him who lives forever and ever, who created heaven and the things that are in it, the earth and the things that are in it, and the sea and the things that are in it,* ***that there should be delay no longer,*** *⁷but in* ***the days of the sounding of the seventh angel,*** *when he is about to sound, the mystery of God would be finished, as He declared to His servants the prophets.*

Daniel 12:7: *Then I heard the* ***man*** *clothed in linen, who was above the waters of the river, when he held up his right hand and his left hand to heaven, and* ***swore*** *by Him who lives forever,* ***that it shall be for a time, times, and half a time;*** *and when the power of the holy people has been completely shattered, all these things shall be finished.*

When are the **"days** ... of the seventh angel?" The book of Daniel gave a clue. The "Man" in **Daniel 12** asked Daniel to "shut up the words" and "seal the book" until the "time of the end." In the book of **Revelation 5,** the book was opened by the Lamb; and the command was given, two thousand years ago, "not to seal" the prophecy of the book in **Revelation 22.** Thus, since the seals of the book are now loosed by the Lamb, and **the seal is the Spirit;**[11] therefore, we through the Spirit can now understand (unseal) times and seasons.

Note: In **Daniel 12:7,** the Man between two angels is a picture of God between the two cherubs. This "Man" (Jesus) was above the waters as the Mighty Angel (Jesus) was above the sea. He also took an oath indicating that "the end" was related to "time, times, and half a time;" and related to scattered holy people. The Messenger in Revelation who stood on the sea (water) and stood the earth took an oath; this time declaring that the interruption of time, as we know it, has begun. "There will be 'uninterrupted time' no longer!"

---

[11] Ephesians 1:13, 1 Corinthians 2:11-12

There is a link. The Holy Spirit can provide us with the times and the seasons of <u>both</u> declarations. Again, in the days of Daniel, "the Man (the Lord) clothed in linen" indicated that it "shall be for **time, times and half a time.**" Several hundred years later, the "Mighty Angel" (Jesus) said there would come **"days"** when there would be **"delay (lit., uninterrupted time) no longer**."

The fact that "days" were not quantified makes the "days" open ended and thus "days" can cover any duration as determined by the Lord's purposes. With that said, we will look at several periods that relates to the time and seasons of the seventh angel with the seventh trumpet to get a sense of the days when the seventh angel sounds. Let us start with some translations of **Daniel 12:7** to get a good understanding of what was said to Daniel.

*Daniel 12:7, Young's Literal Translation: "… 'After a time, times, and a half, and **at the completion of the scattering of the power of the holy people,** finished are all these.'"*

*Daniel 12:7, Darby: … It is for a time, times, and a half; and **when the scattering of the power of the holy people shall be accomplished,** all these things shall be finished*

*Daniel 12:7, NAU: … It would be for a time, times, and half a time; and **as soon as they finish shattering the power of the holy people,** all these events will be completed*

*Daniel 12:7, New Jerusalem Bible: "… "A time and two times, and half a time; and all these things will come true, **once the crushing of the holy people's power is over.'"***

*Daniel 12:7, New Living Translation: … "It will go on for a time, times, and half a time. **When the shattering of the holy people has finally come to an end,** all these things will have happened."*

*Daniel 12:7, ASV: … It shall be for a time, times, and a half; **and when they have made an end of breaking in pieces the power of the holy people,** all these things shall be finished.*

Septuagint (LXX), Rahlfs: That into the set time, and set times and half of-set time the completion of-hands of-sending-away of-people of-holy also shall-be-complete all these

It appears to me that most translations read a little different from the translation given by the New King James and some others. Most of the translation including the Septuagint, the Bible translation quoted by Jesus, Paul, Peter, etc. all indicates that the times, times and half a time being completed is linked to when the holy people will <u>no longer</u> be pushed around (scattered or shattered).

This is how the Hebrew interlinear text reads: *"when is concluded dispersing hand of the people of holiness, conclusion of all these."* Thus, the conclusion of all the things which Daniel saw was linked to the holy people not been shattered or scattered as they used to be. This ties in beautifully with the Mighty Angel's declaration in **Revelation 10:6-7;** and what follows in **Revelation 10:8 through Revelation 11:19.**

The Angel declared that **"there will be time ("chronos— uninterrupted time") no longer."** This "time no longer," through which the mystery of God being completed is linked to the Church (or the firstfruit Christ, the two witnesses) rising from her passive state of being dispersed by disunity and manmade religion, becoming conquerors corporately, not just individually. This empowerment of the witnesses of the Church of Jesus will again happen during "the time, times and half a time" or the 1260 days **(Revelations 11; Revelation 12).**

The uninterrupted duration of time, times and half a time will be interrupted by a holy people who will no longer be pushed around, shattered, or scattered by the world (systems) and the beast that run the world system. The Man (Jesus) in Daniel took an oath; and concluded the same oath in **Revelation 10:6-7.** There will be uninterrupted time no longer! Why?

The seventh angel will interrupt time because of his maturity. The messengers of the gospel (apostles, prophets, teachers, evangelists, pastors, mature saints) will no longer be scattered by the world system. The mystery of God being completed will also interrupt time; because the saints will finally come to the place where Christ in them is now releasing His glory through them; and the Church fulfilling **John 17:21-23.**

That is, the saints (the holy people) will no longer be scattered or shattered by the disunity of some serving the world system, the beast, and then attempting to serve God at the same time. Elijah called this phenomenon a "falter between two opinions" **(1 Kings 18:21).** If the "mystery of God being completed" is understood as linked to Daniel's "time, times and half a time;" then let us look at some other meanings of the **"days** of the seventh angel."

Here is some history to show how awesome the Lord is in His timing. The words given to Daniel in **Daniel 9** through **Daniel 12** were given approximately 3500 years from Adam. The Angel Gabriel appeared to Daniel in **Daniel 9** at the end of the 70 years of Babylonian captivity and approximately 490 years to 500 years before Christ. Jesus' birth was around 4000 years from Adam. By subtracting the approximately 490 to 500 years from 4000 years you get approximately 3500 years from Adam to Daniel visions. "Time, times and a half a time" is seen in 3500 years from Adam to Daniel; and "time, times and a half a time" is also seen from Daniel to the end of the seventh millennium.

"Time, times and half a time" can be understood as 1000 years (time), 2000 years (times) and 500 years (half-a-time). Thus, time, times, and half-a-time from when the "Man" in linen told Daniel that it would be for time, times, and half-a-time, puts the "approximate" completion at the end of 7000 years from Adam (3500 years for Adam to Daniel's vision, plus 3500 years from Daniel's vision adds up to be the end of the 7000 years from Adam).

The "half a time" is approximately 500 years from Daniel to Jesus. The "times," is from Jesus until the end of this age, 2000 years. The "time" is the millennium as outlined in **Revelation 20.** We are now in the **overlap** between "times" (2000 years from Christ to now) and "time" (1000 years reign of the first resurrection saints ruling with Christ).

The days of the sounding of the seventh trumpet were referenced in **Revelation 10:6** before **Revelation 11:1,** and the seventh trumpet was also declared in **Revelation 11:15** to have already sounded, after **Revelation 11:11-14** occurred. **Revelation 11:1** appears to have occurred just at the end of the 2000 years Church age as referenced by the placement of the "Altar" (of Incense) in the tabernacle built by Moses, or just at the beginning of the millennium as understood by the measuring of the "temple of God."[12] **Revelation 11:11** also appears to happen just before the beginning of the millennium of the first resurrection saints who rule <u>with</u> Christ, as exemplified by the "two olive trees." This is understood in conjunction of the placement of the two cherubs made of olive trees in the temple built by Solomon.

Thus, the sounding of the seventh trumpet in **Revelation 11:15** is associated with the "change" of the ages and the change of which God's kingdom rule effective <u>in lieu</u> of the world's kingdom. That is, the seventh trumpet declared that **"the kingdom of the world has become the kingdom of our Lord and His Christ; and He shall reign forever and ever."**

We are in the **overlap**[13] of the ages (the ending of the 6th millennium and the eventual beginning of the 7th millennium where the first resurrection saints rule with Christ). This may last from 33 years (relative to Jesus' age at His ascension), or up to 500 years as seen in Goliath's "span" beyond his six cubits stature.

Also note that "time, times and half-a-time can be 7000 years; 2000 years (time), 4000 years(times) and 1000 years (half-a-time). "Times" (4000 years) happened from Adam to Jesus. "Time"

---

[12] The dimension of the Most Holy Place in the tabernacle built by Moses is 10x10x10=1,000 cubits. This 1,000 cubits points to the 1,000-year reign of Christ in Revelation 20.
[13] See my books *The Last Hour, The First Hour, The 42nd Generation.*

started from Jesus; and it is continuing in this present time to last for approximately 2000 years. "Half-a time" is the Sabbath millennium (1000 years).

Here is another principle: Around each one-thousand-year cycle, God "places" a "son" in the earth. Or as my mentor, who became as a father to me, Dr. Varner said, **"every two thousand years God has a son."** After some research of my own, I found out that Dr. Varner's principle also applies to each one-thousand-year cycle.

Noah was "placed" as a "son" approximately 1000 years form when Adam was created **(Genesis 5:28-29)**. Approximately 1000 years later Isaac the promised "son" was "placed" **(Genesis 18:1)**. One thousand (1000) years later another son was "placed," David **(Psalm 2:7);** and in the fullness of time, approximately 1000 years after David, "the Son" — Jesus — was placed **(Mark 1:11)**.

We are now 2000 years from Jesus, and a corporate "son-male" shall be birth or shall be formed in a people through the Church of our Lord Jesus Christ **(Revelation 12:5)**. This male-son (a company of sons according to **Isaiah 66:7-8 and Exodus 4:22)** was birthed in the days of the voice of the seventh angel whenever he intends to sound, which is around 2000 years from Christ. This is the age we now live in.

Revelation 12:1; 2; 5: ¹Now a great sign appeared in heaven: a woman ... ²... being with child, she cried out in labor and in pain to give birth ... ⁵She bore a male Child ....

Isaiah 66:7-8: ⁷... She delivered a male child. ⁸... For as soon as Zion was in labor, she gave birth to her children (lit. sons).

Exodus 4:22, KJV: And you shall say to Pharaoh, Thus says the LORD, Israel is my son, even my firstborn

Galatians 4:19: My little children, for whom I labor in birth again until Christ is formed in you

A corporate son shall be birthed by the woman, the Church. As surely as Noah, (a son of "comfort") was born and commissioned, as surely as Isaac (the promised son) was born and commissioned, as surely as David (an endorsed son) was born and commissioned, and as surely as Jesus (the Beloved Son) was birthed and commissioned in 1000 years interval, so likewise approximately 2000 years from Jesus, a corporate "male-son" shall be birth through "the incorruptible seed of the Word," through the "hyper" intercession of the Jesus, through the "hyper-intersession" of the Holy Spirit, and through the birth pains of His Holy apostles.

If you are reading this book, you are in the seasons of the corporate male-son being birth by the Church of Jesus Christ, which practically means that Christ will be formed (morphed) in us through the hyper intersession of Jesus, the Holy Spirit, and His apostles who "labor in birth," etc. The fact that you are birthed around 2000 years from Jesus makes you a candidate to be part of the corporate male-son.

With that said, **Revelation 12:6** with **Revelation 12:14** shows that times, time, and a half-a-time can also be 1260 days, or 42 months (3 ½ years). Thus, in **Daniel 12:7,** the angel said that the power of the holy people will no longer be shattered or scattered is linked to "time, times and half-a time" cited in **Revelation 12.**

The seasons of the mystery of God being completed (Jesus Christ being formed or matured in us) is during a season of 1260 days, or 42 months, or 3 ½ years; thus, the Mighty Angel's declaration that there will be "'uninterrupted time' no longer." Chronos will be interrupted by the set season of 1260 days. The days of the seventh angels is linked to the 1260 days, (time=360 days, times=720 days, and half-a-time=180 days).

We must also understand that **Joshua, Chapter 6** is a type of the seven angels with their seven trumpets sounding. In **Joshua 6, all seven trumpets** sounded the entire time they circled the city once each day for six days. On the seventh day, the seven trumpets sounded during the seven trips around the city each of the seven times. Thus, on the seventh day, the priests' trumpets sounded seven times more than the previous six days. This understanding links to the fact that the Greek tense for the angels "trumpeting" in Revelation is in the **"aorist tense."**

In the book of **Revelation 8** through **Revelation 11**, the "trumpeting" of the seven angels are all written in the "aorist tense." Aorist tense has several meanings; the aorist tense points to an event that happened in the past with on-going results. The aorist tense is a snapshot of an event that happened, and that event is continuing. Aorist as also defined to mean an event occurred (in the past), with **no limits as to duration** of that event, and **no limits as to that event repeating** itself.

Thus, the trumpeting of the seven trumpets in the book of Joshua typifies the aorist tense. All seven priests sounded their trumpets for each of the six days: and then on the seventh day the same trumpets **"repeated"** the trumpeting sevenfold more. The angels in the book of Revelation will sound their trumpets individually; however, because they are written in the aorist tense, this means that the seven trumpets have sounded as John saw and wrote; the seven trumpets are sounding; the seven trumpets will sound; and they may repeat themselves, as the Lord wills. In other words, the effects of the seven trumpets are past, present, and future.

Thus, like **Joshua 6,** I believe that during the first six days (first six millenniums from Adam) all seven trumpets occurred uniquely. And as all of Joshua's seven trumpets sounded seven times on the seventh day; it appears that early during the seventh millennium[14], the seven trumpets will sound again. It is also true that from the days John received the Revelation of Jesus Christ, the seven trumpets sounded, is sounding and shall sound.

With that said, **Revelation 5:6** coupled with **2 Chronicles 9:18** also provide a hint about the "days" of the seventh angel. For example, Solomon's throne in **2 Chronicles** is related to **Revelation 5:6 — the Lamb in the middle of the Throne.** Let us take a look.

---

[14] Trumpets sounded on the first day of the 7th Month, so likewise on the first day (~33 years) of the 7th Millennium trumpets will sound.

*2 Chronicles 9:17-18, KJV: Moreover, the king made a **great throne** ... there were **six steps to the throne**, with **a footstool** of gold ....*

Solomon's throne is a symbol of God's throne with the Lamb in the middle of the Throne, as seen in the book of **Revelation 5**. This correlation of Solomon's throne with the Throne of God and the Lamb gives us a glimpse into the times and season of **Revelation 5** and thus **Revelation 8** relative to the seven trumpets.

In Solomon's throne, there was a **footstool** of gold for his throne. "Footstool" is the Hebrew word **"KBSh."** **"KBSh"** is also translated as **"lamb"** in **Leviticus 9:3** and **Ezekiel 46:13**.

The phrase in **2 Chronicles 9:18** could read, *"And there were **six steps to the throne**, with **a 'lamb' of gold [glory]**."* Thus, in the Footstool of God's Throne, there is Jesus, the glorified Lamb that was slain for us, as pictured in **Revelation 5:6**.

*Revelation 5:6: And I beheld, and, lo, **in the midst of the throne** ... **stood a Lamb as it had been slain**, having seven horns and seven eyes,"* which are, *"the Seven Spirits of God sent forth into all the earth.*

Solomon's great ivory throne with its footstool is a type of the Throne of God with "the Lamb" of God in the middle. "And there were ... **the throne**, with **a 'lamb'** of gold [glory]." "Lo, **in the midst of the throne** ... stood a **Lamb** as it had been slain."

Thus, Solomon's throne with the Lamb provides a glimpse into the times and seasons just before the seventh trumpet, relative to the potential times and seasons of **Revelation 4** and **Revelation 5** and consequently **Revelation 6 through Revelation 11**. The approximate times to the "footstool (or the Lamb)" are **"six steps."** *And "there were **six steps to the throne**, with **a footstool (or lit., a Lamb)** of gold (glory)."*

Thus, the time and the seasons of **Revelation 5** (the Throne with the Lamb in the middle of it) may be approximately **six thousand years** from Adam. This is understood by equating each **"step"** of

Solomon's throne to be equal to **1,000 years.** "Step" in this reference is defined as a "journey to a higher place."

We have come **"six steps" (six thousand years)** from the "lower place" of death caused by the first Adam to the "higher place" of life-producing through Jesus, the Lamb of God who is in the middle of the Throne of Grace. It follows that **Revelation 8** with the seven trumpets occurs after the six steps of six thousand years, or just inside the seventh millennium reckoning times from the first Adam.

Another note as to the period of the seven angels with the seven trumpets can be found in **Revelation 8. Revelation 8:1-4** is a picture of the Day of Atonement when the High priest went into the Holy of Holies with incense in the seventh month on the tenth day of each year **(Leviticus 16 w/Leviticus 23).**

If we divide each 1000-year period by 12 months or 7 months (every seven month there is a Sabbath cycle looking at the Hebrew "sacred" and "civil" calendar together), this puts the seven trumpets to start sounding around the **early** 1500s (Martin Luther Reformation), or around the early 1900s (Azusa Street Revival).

Here is another picture. According to the set times for the feasts of the Lord in **Leviticus 23:24,** the first day of the "seventh" month is a "day" of "trumpets blasts." The fact that **Revelation 8:2; 8:6-7** mentioned the trumpets and them being sounded (blasted) also puts the time for the sounding of the seven trumpets at the beginning of the seventh month. Thus, on the first day (33 years) of each millennium; especially, the first day of the seventh millennium trumpets (plural) will be sounding.

The trumpet may also last for the entire Sabbath millennium. The seventh trumpet is the last trumpet. The "seventh (last) trumpet" sounding in **Revelation 10:6** is the beginning of the days of the last trumpet. The **"last** trumpet" sounding in **1 Corinthians 15: 52** is the **"farthest"** of "place or **time"** of the seventh trumpet – one thousand years after the seventh (last) angel began trumpeting.

This one thousand years sounding of the seventh or last trumpet is implied prophetically by the "days" leading up to Jesus transfiguration, which "transfiguration" Jesus calls his **"coming** in His kingdom."** Peter also calls Jesus transfiguration "Jesus power and **coming" (Matthew 16:28, 2 Peter 1:16-18, Matthew 17:1-2, Luke 9:28-29, 2 Peter 3:8;** you may also refer to my book *Jesus' Resurrection, Our Inheritance,* chapter 4, for further explanation).

These trumpets sounding may range anywhere from two trumpets sounding at a time, to all seven angels trumpeting with their seven trumpets. According to the worlds timetable, we are in a new millennium, which places us at the start of seven thousand years from Adam. In the new millennium, the first day (33 years) is a day of trumpets. **Note though:** The Lord and His Church is now the timetable[15] as ascertained from the "Tent of Time" in heaven that Moses copied exactly **(Hebrews 8:5).**

With that said, be mindful that the Bible did not define "explicitly" the durations of the sounding of most of the trumpets. The days of the first trumpet, the second trumpet, and the third trumpet are not defined. The fourth trumpet <u>may be</u> for a day and a night by extrapolation.

The days of the fifth trumpet were defined as "five months," which the Bible defines as the days of hiding. The sixth trumpet may last for thirteen month and twenty-five hours. With that said, here is a truth as revealed by the Holy Spirit: the sixth angel also has the authority to sound his trumpet to release his plague for "the hour" if God chooses; for "a month" if God chooses; for "a day" period if God chooses; or for "a year" period if God chooses.

The seventh angel's trumpet sounds will last for "days" (these days may be for 1260 days?). The use of "days" makes the duration of the "days" of the seventh angel open ended. We know that the use of "days" makes his sounding more than one day. However, how many days after the first day are unknown? (These days may

---

[15]The duration of the Church age starts after Jesus' death, burial, and resurrection (~33 years)

be for 1260 days?). With that said, I know I have given several scenarios when theses trumpets may sound, could sound, or shall be sounding. **Yet, here is a reality check!**

Do we really know when? Remember after Daniel asked the Man to explain to him *"How long will it be before these astonishing things are fulfilled"* of what was shown to Daniel **(Daniel 12:6, NIV).** The Man **did answer** Daniel; *"that it shall be for a time, times, and half a time" (Daniel 12:7).*

Yet, Daniel still left the angel saying: ***"I heard, but I did not understand" (Daniel 12: 8, NIV).***

Who are the Seven Angels?

*Revelation 8:2: And I saw the **seven angels** who stand before God, and to them were given seven trumpets.*

*Revelation 1:20: The mystery of **the seven stars** which you saw in My right hand, and the seven golden lampstands: **The seven stars are the angels of the seven churches**, and the seven lampstands which you saw are the seven churches.*

There are indeed seven angels that stand before God. According to the **Talmud, they are *Michael, Gabriel, Raphael, and Uriel;*** and according to **1 Enoch 20,** there is *Michael, Gabriel, Raphael, Uriel, Raguel, Saraqâêl, and Remiel.*

Here are the meanings of their names. Michael, "he who is like God;" Gabriel, "man of God;" Raphael, "healer of God;" Uriel, "fire of God;" Raguel, "shepherd or friend of God;" Saraqâêl, "command of God;" and Remiel, "thunder of God." Michael, the archangel is found in the book of **Daniel, Jude,** and **Revelation.** Gabriel is found in **Daniel** and **Luke.** Raphael is found in the Apocryphal books in the book of **Tobit 12:15.** Michael is indeed called an "archangel" or "one of the chief angels."

Yet the angels in Revelations, including but not limited to the seven angels, has other applications. The Lord, Himself said that the "stars" in His hands were "angels of the seven Churches." These angels are the overseers of the Church. One must also realize that the words spoken by the Lord in **Revelation 2** thru **Revelation 3** were spoken directly to the "angel of [that] Church." These seven angels are **also** symbols of all the messengers of the Church of Jesus Christ. These messengers are apostles, prophets, teachers, evangelist, and pastors. How can a single angel represent many messengers?

In **Revelation 7:2-3** we learn that the "angel" (singular)" is really **many** angels, **"we."** "I saw **another angel** ascending from the east, having the seal of the living God. And he cried with a loud voice … 'Do not harm … till **we** have sealed the servants of our God on their foreheads.'" As one can see, the **"we"** are the **"another angel."**

Also, our Lord did not address the Church members themselves until towards the end of each of His discourse. The language tells the reader that the "angels" are human beings. As one read all the words that were spoken to the angels we can see that **one of these angels was married** (see below). **Angels in heaven do not marry (Luke 20:35-36).** But the angels of the earth can.

Revelation 2:18-20: ¹⁸*"And to the **angel** of the church in Thyatira write, 'These things says the Son of God, who has eyes like a flame of fire, and His feet like fine brass:* ¹⁹*"I know your works, love, service, faith, and your patience; and as for your works, the last are more than the first.* ²⁰*"Nevertheless I have a few things against you, because you allow **that woman (lit., the wife of-you)** Jezebel, who calls herself a prophetess, to teach and seduce."*

The angel of the Church of Thyatira had a **wife**. Her name was Jezebel. And as Jesus said, angels in heaven do not marry or are given in marriage. Thus, the angel of Thyatira was a human. Here is another example of angels being men.

Revelation 22:8-9: ⁸*Now I, John, saw and heard these things. And when I heard and saw, I fell down to **worship before the feet of the angel** who showed me these things.* ⁹ *Then he said to me, "See that you do not do that. **For I am your fellow servant, and of your brethren the prophets,** and of those who keep the words of this book. Worship God."*

In the verses above see John, the beloved apostle wanted to worship the angel that showed him some things that occurred after the seven angels poured out their bowls of wrath. In fact, it was on the angels who poured out the bowls of wrath that John tried to worship. **"I fell down to worship before the feet of the angel who showed me these things."** However, the angel had a surprise for John. First: the angel would not allow "angel worship." Instead, the angel said, **"Worship God!"** Second: the angel was **"of the prophets."**

Yes, the angels that poured out the bowls of wraths are "prophets" (humans); they are also called "slaves" of the Lord; and they are also called "of those who keep the words of this book" (the book of Revelation). Thus, we see that "prophets" are called "angels" **(see also Haggai 1:13)**. The angels that Jesus referenced in **John 1:51** appears to be also humans who originated from the earth seen in the fact that the "ascended" first, before they "descended."

*John 1:51: And He said to him, "Most assuredly, I say to you, hereafter you shall see heaven open, and the **angels of God ascending and descending** upon the Son of Man."*

*Genesis 28:12: Then [Jacob] dreamed, and behold, a **ladder** was set up on the **earth,** and its top reached to heaven; and there the angels of God were **ascending and descending** on it.*

The angels in described by Jesus did **not** start their journey in heaven, same as the ones that Jacob saw at the ladder in **Genesis 28:12.** How did I know this? Dr. Turnel Nelson taught that Jesus did **not** say these angels would be first descending and then ascending. On the contrary, these "angels of God" would be "ascending" from the earth, as Jacob saw them ascending from the earth, to hear a message from God and then "descending" back to the earth to disburse their message.

Remember that Paul, an apostle also called himself an "angel of God;" and Paul ascended and descended between third heaven and earth **(2 Corinthians 12:1-4).** The apostle John also migrated between heaven and earth **(Revelation 4:1-2)** Jesus himself said that He was on earth and in heaven at the same time **(John 3:13).**

As I indicated earlier in this book, John the Baptist, whom Jesus credited as the greatest prophet who lived, was called a "messenger (lit., angel)." Our Lord Himself is called "the Messenger." Think it not strange that apostles and prophets are also called angels. Again, Paul, an apostle also called himself an "angel of God."

*Galatians 4:14: And my trial which was in my flesh you did not despise or reject, but you received me as an **angel of God,** even as **Christ Jesus.***

Two things can be taken from the verse above that is full of spiritual understanding. Paul said the Church of Galatia receive him as Christ Jesus. This should not be strange; since the body of believers who have been baptized into Christ in the Holy Spirit "is the Christ." "For as the body is one and has many members, but all the members of that one body, being many, are one body, **so also is 'the' Christ**. For by one **Spirit,** we were all baptized into one body" **(1 Corinthians 12:12-13).**

The same is true concerning Paul being received as an "angel of God." Jesus, His holy Apostles, and prophets for sure are also called angels; and apostles and prophets are among the angels in the book of Revelation who release the judgments of God in the waters, earth, air, etc. As we learned in a previous chapter, "priests," among others are also called angels. Let us review what was said in a previous chapter.

Jesus calls His apostles angels **(Luke 9:52-54).** The Bible calls prophets "angels;" and priests are also called messengers (lit., angels) **(Malachi 2:7).** The prophet Malachi called John, the Baptist an angel. Malachi also called Jesus "the Angel."

*Malachi 3:1: "Behold, I send **My messenger**, and he will prepare the way before Me. And the Lord, whom you seek, will suddenly come to His temple, even the **Messenger of the covenant,** in whom you delight. Behold, He is coming," Says the LORD of hosts.*

*Luke 7:26-28: [26]But what went ye out to see? a prophet? Yea, I say unto you, and much more than a prophet. [27]This is he of whom it is written, Behold, I send **my messenger** before thy face, who shall prepare thy way before thee. [28] I say unto you, among them that are born of women there is none greater than **John:** yet he that is but little in the kingdom of God is greater than he.*

It is clear from the references that "my messenger" is John, the Baptist, as also witnessed by the Lord Jesus Himself. In addition, "the Messenger of the Covenant" is Jesus, whom Malachi called "the Lord." *"And **the Lord** who you seek ... even **the Messenger** of the covenant."* Jesus is the Lord. Jesus is also "the Angel who suddenly came to His temple."

Paul referring to himself as "an angel of God" appears to be linked to the seven angels with the seven trumpets. It appears to me that the seven angels with the seven trumpets are "prophetic apostles," and "apostolic prophets." Paul said, *"You received me as an **angel of God"** (Galatians 4:14).* John "saw the **seven angels** who stand before **God** and to them were given seven **trumpets" (Revelation 8:2).** *"The angel ... said ... I am your fellow **servant**, and of your brethren **the prophets"** (Revelation 22:8-9).*

Paul called himself an "angel of God." These seven "angels" stood before "God." They were given trumpets which symbolizes the prophetic ministry according to **Ezekiel 33:1-7.** The angel in **Revelation 22** also called himself a prophet. Thus, the seven angels include apostles ("sent messengers") of God with a prophetic word, who can be called, "prophetic apostles." They also include "apostolic prophets" sent with prophetic words. The five-fold ministries (apostles, prophets, teachers, evangelist, and pastors) can sometimes function in dual offices. That is, legitimate sons' functions in all the offices as the Father wills it to be.

Peter was a pastoral apostle. Jesus said that John, the Baptist, was an "apostolic prophet" (a prophet with apostolic overtone). John, the beloved was a "prophetic apostle" (an apostle that is prophetic). Paul was a prophetic-apostle, preacher-apostle, and a teacher-apostle.

Concerning John, the Baptist Jesus said that John, the Baptist was *"**much more than a prophet**. This is he of whom it is written, Behold, I send (lit., **apostello**) my messenger" (Luke 7:26-27).* John was "much more than a prophet." Thus, he was an apostolic ("sent") prophet.

We know that Peter is one of the apostles of the Lamb **(Luke 6:13-14).** Yet Peter was called a "shepherd" in **John 21:16.** "He said to him again a second time, "Simon, son of Jonah, do you love Me?"

He said to Him, "Yes, Lord; You know that I love You." He said to him, **"Tend (lit., shepherd) My sheep."** Therefore, one can conclude that Peter is a pastoral apostle **(1 Peter 5:1-4).** Paul (formerly Saul) was a prophet before he was "dispatched" as an apostle. He was also a teacher.

1 Timothy 2:7: For which I was appointed **a preacher** *and* **an apostle** — *I am speaking the truth in Christ and not lying* — **a teacher** *of the Gentiles in faith and truth.*

Acts 13:1: Now in the church that was at Antioch there were certain **prophets and teachers:** *Barnabas, Simeon who was called Niger, Lucius of Cyrene, Manaen who had been brought up with Herod the tetrarch, and* **Saul.**

We have seen that the seven angels of the seven Churches are the overseers of the Church **(Revelation 1:20).** We also learn that the seven angels with the seven bowls are prophets who came out of the temple of God (the Church) **(Revelation 15:6 w/Revelation 22:8-9).**

The seventh angel trumpet (message) also includes a conclusion of the "mystery of God" as revealed to His "servants **the prophets.**" According to Paul, the revelation of the mystery of Christ is given to God's holy apostles and prophets by the Holy Spirit and "the prophetic Scriptures" of the prophets.

1 Peter 1:10: Of this salvation, the **prophets** *have inquired and searched carefully,* **who prophesied** *of the grace that would come to you.*

Romans 16:25-26: [25]Now to Him who is able to establish you according to my gospel and the **preaching of Jesus Christ, according to the revelation of the mystery** *kept secret since the world began [26]But now has been made manifest, and by the* **prophetic Scriptures** *has been made known to all nations, according to the commandment of the everlasting God, for obedience to the faith.*

Ephesians 3:3-5: [3]How that by revelation He made known to me the mystery (as I have briefly written already, [4]by which, when you read, you may understand my knowledge in **the mystery of Christ),** *[5]which in* *other ages was not made known to the sons of men, as it has now been* **revealed by the Spirit** *to His* **holy apostles and prophets:**

Thus, the seventh angel; with his seventh trumpet, along with the rest of the six angels, with their six trumpets, are at a minimum apostles and prophets. John, an apostle was said to be **"of"** the prophets. John was also called a "fellow" brother among the prophets. The angel (a prophet) said to John, "I am your fellow servant, and **of your brethren** the prophets" **(Revelation 22:9).**

The bowls of wrath that was poured out on mystery Babylon was the judgment of the apostles and prophets. According to the Old and New Testament, apostles and prophets and **mature** saints can give directive words, predictive words, and judgments.

Revelation 18:20, Young's Literal Translation: 'Be glad over her, O heaven, and ye holy **apostles and prophets,** *because God did judge* **your judgment** *of her!'*

Revelation 18:20, ASV: Rejoice over her, thou heaven, and **ye saints,** *and* **ye apostles, and ye prophets;** *for God hath judged* **your judgment** *on her.*

Finally, think it not strange that ministers can walk in multiple offices, including "as angels." Jesus is our pattern. In the Scriptures, Jesus is "the Angel of the (New) Covenant;" Jesus is "the Apostle;" He is the "High Priests;" He is the Great Priest, He is "the Prophet;" Jesus is "the Evangelist;" He is "the Teacher," Jesus is the "Great Shepherd (Pastor) of the sheep." Jesus is "King of kings and Lord of lords." Yes! Jesus is Lord!

Other Books

Wisdom from Above, by Judith Peart
Procreation, Understanding Sex, and Identity, by Judith Peart
100 Nevers, by Judith Peart
The Shattered and the Healing by Judith Peart
The Lamb, by Donald Peart
Jesus' Resurrection, Our Inheritance, by Donald Peart.
Sexuality, By Donald Peart
Forgiven 490 Times, by Donald Peart w/Judith Peart!
The Days of the Seventh Angel, By Donald Peart
The Torah (The Principle) of Giving, by Donald Peart
The Time Came, by Donald Peart
The Last Hour, the First Hour, the Forty-Second Generation, by Donald Peart
Vision Real, by Donald Peart
The False Prophet, Alias, Another Beast V1, by Donald Peart
"the beast," by Donald Peart
Son of Man Prophesy Against the false prophet, by Donald Peart
The Dragon's Tail, the Prophets who Teach Lies, by Donald Peart
The Work of Lawlessness Revealed, by Donald Peart
When the Lord Made the Tempter, by Donald Peart
Examining Doctrine, Volume 1, by Donald Peart
Exousia, Your God Given Authority, by Donald Peart
The Numbers of God, by Donald Peart
The Completions of the Ages … by Donald Peart
The Revelation of Jesus Christ, by Donald Peart
Jude—Translation and Commentary, by Donald Peart
Obtaining the Better Resurrection, by Donald Peart
Manifestations from Our Lord Jesus ...by Donald and Judith Peart).
Obtaining the Better Resurrection, by Donald Peart
The New Testament, Dr. Donald Peart Exegesis
The Tree of Life, By Dr. Donald Peart
The Spirit and Power of John, the Baptist by Dr. Donald Peart
The Shattered and the Healing by Judith Peart
Is She Married to a Husband? by Donald Peart
The Ugliest Man God Made by Donald Peart
Does Answering the Call of God Impact Your Children? by Donald Peart
Victory Out-of-the Beast-the Harvest of the Earth by Donald Peart
The Order of Melchizedek by Donald Peart

Ezekiel-the House-the City-the Land (Interpreting the Patterns), by Donald Peart
Butter and Honey, Understanding how to Choose the Good and Refuse Evil, by Donald Peart

Contact Information:

Crown of Glory Ministries
P.O. Box 1041 Randallstown, MD 21133
donaldpeart7@gmail.com

About the Author:

Donald Peart is married to Judith Peart since 1986. They believe that Jesus is the Christ, the Son of the living God; and they preach the gospel of God's kingdom centered on Jesus Christ. They have founded and currently oversee Crown of Glory Ministries in Randallstown, Maryland. Donald and his wife have written over 35 books; and their ministry has distributed their books to at least 29 States in the USA and 21 countries. Donald has earned an Associate of Arts degree in Pre-Engineering, a Bachelor of Science degree in Civil Engineering. He also earned a Master of Divinity, a Master of Science in Construction Management, and a Doctorate in Theology.

www.ingramcontent.com/pod-product-compliance
Lightning Source LLC
Chambersburg PA
CBHW032214040426
42449CB00005B/593